CHIHUAHUA

LINDA BOLLINGER

Chihuahua

Editor: Heather Russell-Revesz
Copy Editor: Joann Woy
Indexer: Lucie Haskins
Series Design: Mary Ann Kahn
Designer: Patricia Escabi

TFH Publications®
President/CEO: Glen S. Axelrod
Executive Vice President: Mark E. Johnson
Editor-in-Chief: Albert Connelly, Jr.
Production Manager: Kathy Bontz

TFH Publications, Inc.®
One TFH Plaza
Third and Union Avenues
Neptune City, NJ 07753

Discovery Communications, Inc. Book Development Team: Marjorie Kaplan, President and General Manager, Animal Planet Media / Kelly Day, EVP and General Manager, Discovery Commerce / Elizabeth Bakacs, Vice President, Licensing and Creative / JP Stoops, Director, Licensing / Bridget Stoyko, Associate Art Director

Copyright © 2011 by TFH Publications, Inc.

Printed and bound in China

13 14 15 16   3 5 7 9 8 6 4 2

Library of Congress Cataloging-in-Publication Data
Bollinger, Linda C.
  Chihuahua / Linda Bollinger.
       p. cm.
  Includes index.
  ISBN 978-0-7938-3716-8 (alk. paper)
  1. Chihuahua (Dog breed) I. Title.
  SF429.C45B65 2011
  636.76--dc22
                                2010052261

This book has been published with the intent to provide accurate and authoritative information in regard to the subject matter within. While every reasonable precaution has been taken in preparation of this book, the author and publisher expressly disclaim responsibility for any errors, omissions, or adverse effects arising from the use or application of the information contained herein. The techniques and suggestions are used at the reader's discretion and are not to be considered a substitute for veterinary care. If you suspect a medical problem consult your veterinarian.

Note: In the interest of concise writing, "he" is used when referring to puppies and dogs unless the text is specifically referring to females or males. "She" is used when referring to people. However, the information contained herein is equally applicable to both sexes.

The Leader In Responsible Animal Care for Over 50 Years!®
www.tfh.com

CONTENTS

ORIGINS OF YOUR CHIHUAHUA

In the history of the Americas, great dramas have been acted out—empires have fallen, races of people have been conquered only to emerge from slavery and evolve into stronger civilizations. And the history of the little Chihuahua occurred right alongside the people going through those turbulent times. The predecessors of the breed were idolized as a spiritual symbol, served as palace companions, eaten as a main course, and driven nearly to extinction, only to finally emerge in their rightful place as a well-loved companion.

Experts in archeology, folklore, and history cannot agree on one true story for the Chihuahua because of the intertwining of fact and unproven myth. Although the breed history may not be as clearly traceable as with some other breeds of dogs, a review of the different theories will paint a picture of the development of the lovable dog we know today.

EARLY HISTORY: A WOLF'S PERSPECTIVE

Before we get into how the Chihuahua breed developed, it's important to understand the history of canine domestication. Scientists accept as true that all modern dogs are the descendants of wolves. Prior to the use of DNA, the history of canines depended on archeology and folklore.

Recent mitochondrial DNA evidence suggests that all the dogs of the world originally came from the Middle East. Previously, it was believed that dogs descended from ancestor animals in Asia. Who knows what will be discovered by archeology and DNA research in the future?

No one knows for certain how exactly dogs were domesticated. One theory about canine development suggests that, when people began practicing agriculture, they used tame wolves not only for hunting but for other tasks as well. These dog ancestors may have been selected for herding and guarding jobs. At that point, these "pre-dogs" would have changed enormously, and a permanent division between dogs and wolves occurred.

As people traveled the globe, dogs went with them, which led to an increase in the numbers of dogs, as well as the continuing demand for specialization. In turn, this created the need for selective breeding in order to create specialized types of dogs and a demand for dogs as pets.

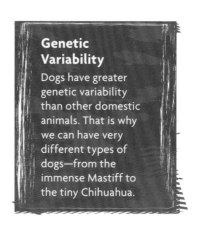

Genetic Variability

Dogs have greater genetic variability than other domestic animals. That is why we can have very different types of dogs—from the immense Mastiff to the tiny Chihuahua.

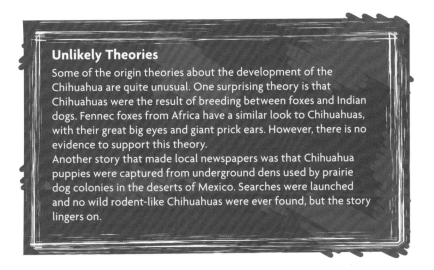

Unlikely Theories

Some of the origin theories about the development of the Chihuahua are quite unusual. One surprising theory is that Chihuahuas were the result of breeding between foxes and Indian dogs. Fennec foxes from Africa have a similar look to Chihuahuas, with their great big eyes and giant prick ears. However, there is no evidence to support this theory.

Another story that made local newspapers was that Chihuahua puppies were captured from underground dens used by prairie dog colonies in the deserts of Mexico. Searches were launched and no wild rodent-like Chihuahuas were ever found, but the story lingers on.

NEOTENY

The rapid evolution of dogs from wolves is an example of *neoteny* (also called *juvenilization*), a subject that is studied by biologists. It means that the adults in a species keep the traits seen only in juveniles of the species. In the case of dogs, the physical development is slowed or delayed, which results in the retention of puppy-like characteristics well into maturity. Dogs shared physical features with the wolf cub, which made them look less threatening than adult wolves and so contributed to their natural (and then later artificial) selection. These physical baby-like characteristics remind humans of our own babies, causing us to feel protective and loving toward them. We see them as helpless and cute.

With Chihuahuas, neoteny goes further than with any other domestic dog breed. Because of their infantile size, large rounded head, and big expressive eyes they are the canine epitome of a human baby.

HISTORY OF THE CHIHUAHUA: FACT AND FICTION

Questions about the origins of the Chihuahua breed would seem to be simple to answer based solely on his name. *Chihuahua* is the name of the biggest state in northern Mexico, so you might assume that's where the breed came from. However, the origin of this breed has been disputed for so long that it's almost impossible to know the truth. There are numerous plausible stories about the history of the Chihuahua, but just like many of our own human histories, there is a suspicion of factual embellishment by the well intended.

THE TECHICHI THEORY

About 11,000 years ago, the Toltecs were a nomadic people who conquered much of Central and South America. The Toltecs were associated with dogs called *Techichi*, small, heavy-bodied, and shaggy-coated dogs. These dogs had a humped back and were not quite as cute as the Chihuahua we know today. They were also most likely mute, for when Columbus came to the New World he described the native people's dogs as small, and unable to bark.

The Techichi was most likely indigenous to Central America as early as the fifth century, which puts them in the right place to contribute to a Chihuahua's heritage. Historical clues and the remains of pyramids found on the Yucatan peninsula means the Techichi may have been living in southeastern Mexico in Chichen Itza. Images of the Techichi carved on stones used in the monastery at Huejotzingo also link the dog to the Toltecs. The carvings of dogs on these stones resemble the Chihuahua.

The Toltecs (and later the Aztecs) considered the Techichi to be a sacred dog and a companion. They were used in religious rituals that both these societies believed in: by burying these dogs with their deceased owners, the person's sins would be transferred to the dog, thus freeing the person of wrongdoings. Techichi then guided the human soul through the underworld, while warding off evil spirits.

Families kept these dogs to be sacrificed and buried with departed family members. Red-colored dogs were favored because the color was considered the primary color of temptation. Guiding a soul through the darkness of the underworld is quite an accomplishment for a dog, even a Chihuahua! The remains of humans and the dogs who had been buried with them have been found in Mexico.

Aztecs

The Aztec people conquered the Toltecs in the 14th century and became the ruling class. The aristocrats and clergy considered the Techichi pets. However, the common people, who were enduring real hardship, added the little dogs to their meals as a source of protein to help them in their hardscrabble existence.

Mayans

The early Mayans of the American continent made clay sculptures of early Chihuahua-like dogs who were portrayed holding stalks of corn in their mouths. This may be symbolic of the Techichi being fattened up for the dinner pot. However, other archaeologists believe that these Mayan sculptures were depictions of rodents—prairie dogs that were raised by the locals to eat, and not actual canines at all!

The Spanish Influence

The Techichi story continues with the Spanish conquerors who invaded Mexico, the Caribbean, and South America. It is speculated that the Spanish had with them small black-and-tan terrier-type dogs who crossed with the Techichi, and the resulting dogs may have been the primitive ancestors of the Chihuahua.

The Spanish Conquistador Fernando Cortez started keeping these little dogs and crossbred them with other canines of small size, which supposedly gave them their smooth coat. The new dogs were also reported to be very vocal, in contrast to the silent Techichi. Soon after the arrival of the Spanish, the original Techichi dogs seem to have vanished.

After the Spanish destroyed the Aztecs in about 1519, Montezuma II, the last Aztec ruler of Mexico, disappeared with his wealth and his little dogs. The dogs were abandoned and left to survive on their own in the wild. The Spanish were rumored to have hunted and eaten most of these dogs, but the natives hid enough of them to allow the breed to survive.

Fennec foxes may slightly resemble Chihuahuas, but there is no truth to the legend that they are related.

Three centuries later, in 1850, the offspring of the Techichi dogs were found by American tourists in the ruins close to Casa Grandes, believed to be the palace that belonged to the Emperor Montezuma the First.

THE EUROPEAN THEORY

It has been suggested that the Chihuahua has an Old World origin, just like European toy dogs. European dogs were prized and developed into lapdogs. Lapdogs are not a breed but rather a type of dog with a manageable disposition and small enough to be held in a lap. Those with leisure time kept lapdogs as companion animals. Lapdogs were the earliest types of dog to live with people in their homes. They were used to lure fleas away from their owners, to provide warmth (much like a primitive heating pad), and some people even believed they could remove illnesses.

Some theorize that it was the Spanish conquistadors who actually brought a small European lapdog with them to the New World. For proof, people who support this theory point to the island of Malta. There, a small breed of dog existed who possessed a natural molera (a soft spot on the top of the skull where three sections of the skull bone should meet). The molera is extremely rare and uncommon to other breeds of dog. Since the Chihuahua possesses this natural molera, it is believed that this points the breed's origins to Malta. Some researchers think the Chihuahua came to the Americas from ships that stopped in Malta and took on board some of the small breed of dog that used to inhabit that island.

However, another theory posits that the opposite is true. The ancient seafarers could have easily picked Chihuahuas up in the New World and taken them back home with them. This would explain why the dogs in Malta had the molera—it was passed on from the New World ancestors of the Chihuahua.

Others in support of the European theory point to the Sistine Chapel in Italy. A painting by Sondro Botticelli, completed in 1482, depicts a dog who looks very much like today's Chihuahua. Since this painting was completed before Columbus sailed for the New World, some authorities support the idea that the Chihuahua is of European ancestry.

MEXICAN BREEDS

Although some may argue European roots, there is a belief that the Chihuahua is actually from a long ancestry of dogs bred in Mexico. Given that folklore and archeology support this view, it may be credible.

While the earliest Chihuahuas were found in Chihuahua, Mexico, the place of origin is more likely to be the entire country rather than only one area. Various types of dogs are known to have existed in pre-Spanish America. These dogs were described in archaeological sources and in the testimonies of the Spaniards. The medium-sized furry type was called the *itzcuintli*, the medium-sized hairless type was called the *xoloitzcuintli*, and the short-legged furry type the *tlalchichi*.

The hairless Xoloitzcuintli, often called the "Mexican Hairless" or "Xolo" (pronounced Zo-lo), is the national of dog of Mexico. Because of the prevalence of hairless dogs in pre-Columbian America, some believe the Chihuahua is a derivative of this hairless breed. However, the Xoloitzcuintli breed is distinctly not the same dog as the Chihuahua. It is possible that a hairless breed contributed to the bloodline of the Chihuahua, but many experts think that the Chinese Crested Dog is more likely.

THE ASIAN THEORY

Some historians believe that the ancestors of the current Chihuahua were hairless dogs brought from Asia in prehistory—through Russia and the Bering Straits to Alaska, and from there south to the American continent. However, hairless dogs have existed in Mexico and South America who are believed to be the ancestors of the modern Xoloitzcuintli. Could the dogs who came from the Bering Strait have been the originators of both the Xolo and the Chihuahua?

Other historians believe that the ancestors of the Chihuahua came from China. The Chinese had successfully miniaturized plants and animals, so it's easy to suppose that when they came from China over 200 years ago, rich merchants

The hairless Xoloitzcuintli, the national dog of Mexico, may have contributed to the bloodline of the Chihuahua.

brought their small dogs with them. But some scientists believe that the Native Americans had dogs in the New World thousands of years before the Chinese sailed to the Americas.

MIXED HERITAGE

One theory of the development of the Chihuahua is that each of these stories has an element of truth. The Chihuahua could be a mixture of several of the dog types from the conflicting stories who were bred together to eventually form one breed—the Chihuahua. It will be up to scientists and historians to unravel the jumbled history of the Chihuahua.

CHIHUAHUA HISTORY IN NORTH AMERICA

In the mid-1800s, tourists bought dogs resembling Chihuahuas from resourceful Mexicans in the areas bordering Mexico, including Arizona and Texas. Thus, these small canines were nicknamed "Mexico dogs," "Texas dogs," or "Arizona dogs." These dogs didn't arouse the general public's interest during those years. The vast majority of people in the United States didn't appreciate or know much about the Chihuahua then.

The Chinese Crested may have also had a part in the Chihuahua past.

The American Kennel Club recognized the Chihuahua in 1904.

In 1888, James Watson, a well-known dog show judge, brought several of these "Mexico dogs" into the United States. He published two articles about the purchase of these dogs, but the stories differed in how he acquired them. Over time, Watson bought several more of the small dogs south of the border. He stated that the dogs he saw had a great variation in body type, coat type, coat color, size, and conformation. However, the one thing that tied the dogs together was that they all had the molera (soft spot) in the skull.

In the late 1800s, interest in dog shows began to increase, and kennel clubs and dog shows were organized. Very small numbers of Chihuahuas were presented in dog shows at that time, and from the 1890s onward, growth of Chihuahua numbers was very sluggish. Many people were keeping Chihuahuas in their homes as pets and "carry-around companions," but they weren't being shown.

In the late 19th century, Owen Wister brought a few of the dogs home after visiting Presidio, Texas, and he decided to name them "Chihuahuas" after the area of Mexico in which they were found. The name stuck, and Chihuahua (or "Chi") is what they are still called today. Chihuahua translates into "dry, sandy place," which describes the original environment the dog lived in.

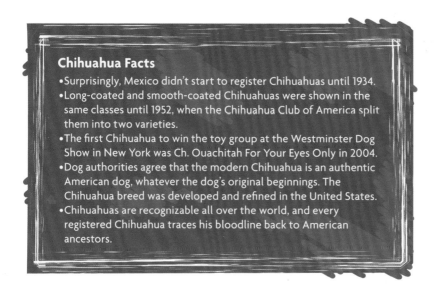

Chihuahua Facts

- Surprisingly, Mexico didn't start to register Chihuahuas until 1934.
- Long-coated and smooth-coated Chihuahuas were shown in the same classes until 1952, when the Chihuahua Club of America split them into two varieties.
- The first Chihuahua to win the toy group at the Westminster Dog Show in New York was Ch. Ouachitah For Your Eyes Only in 2004.
- Dog authorities agree that the modern Chihuahua is an authentic American dog, whatever the dog's original beginnings. The Chihuahua breed was developed and refined in the United States.
- Chihuahuas are recognizable all over the world, and every registered Chihuahua traces his bloodline back to American ancestors.

THE AMERICAN KENNEL CLUB

Founded in 1884, the American Kennel Club (AKC) is the foremost registry of purebred dog pedigrees in the United States. It is the largest purebred dog registry in the world. In addition to maintaining pedigrees, the AKC sanctions and promotes events for purebred dogs, including the annual Westminster Kennel Club dog show and the Eukanuba National Championship dog show. The AKC also advocates for purebred dogs and canine health; it works to protect the rights of owners and educates the public about responsible dog ownership.

The AKC recognized the Chihuahua in 1904, which makes the Chihuahua an old breed by American standards. The first Chi registered in the AKC Stud Book in 1904 was named Midget, bred and owned by H. Raynor from Texas. Midget's littermate Bonito was also registered and, along with three other dogs bred by H. Raynor, are the ancestors to the modern Chihuahua.

In 1904, only 11 Chihuahuas were shown in the whole of the United States. Twelve years later, only 50 dogs were shown. From then, the popularity of the Chihuahua increased steadily.

THE CHIHUAHUA CLUB OF AMERICA

Every breed recognized by a national club like the AKC has a parent club (or breed club). The breed club consists of a group of people who write the breed standard, which is a written description that defines that breed. The Chihuahua

The Chihuahua Club of America is the parent club for the breed.

Club of America (CCA) is the association of Chihuahua fanciers who wrote and continue to preserve the Chihuahua standard. The CCA provides information to the public about the Chihuahua, and its members adhere to a code of ethics overseen by the club. The CCA sponsors dog competitions and other events related to the breed. They promote the health of the Chihuahua and the qualities of the breed through educational seminars, publications, and data banks.

The CCA breed standard was formalized in 1923 and has seen only minor revisions since then. The following year, a Chi named "Beppie," a fawn and white colored dog, was the breed's first champion.

THE CHIHUAHUA TODAY

In the 20th century, U.S. breeders developed the Chihuahua into the modern dog we know. Breeders worked to achieve the Chihuahua you see in today's dog shows and homes by sticking to the breed standard guidelines written by the CCA.

The Chihuahua is a favorite pet of many people around the globe. Don't believe that the Chihuahua's popularity is new—people have treasured the Chihuahua (or a version of him) for centuries. However, in recent years, Chihuahuas have become celebrities in their own right, appearing frequently in movies and advertising. The Chihuahua is such a colorful character, it's no wonder he has become an object of interest for celebrities and everyday people alike.

CHARACTERISTICS OF YOUR CHIHUAHUA

Why do people love Chihuahuas? Could it be their expressive faces? The boys look like a wisecracking street-smart character; the girls look like a flirtatious belle, batting their lashes over those big brown eyes. Could it be their personalities? Cheerful dogs, they keep themselves and everyone around them smiling. There are as many reasons for the Chihuahua's popularity as there are Chihuahuas.

Affectionate, attractive, and greatly loyal, the American Kennel Club (AKC) classifies the Chihuahua as a member of the Toy Group. Members of this group are bred specifically to be companions, and as such, Chihuahuas arguably do the best job of any companion animal out there.

PHYSICAL CHARACTERISTICS

Chihuahuas are a pretty picture, with their distinctive apple head, large luminous dark eyes, and flared ears. These are charming and bright, diminutive yet graceful dogs who have a distinct allure. Let's take a look at what an "ideal" Chihuahua should look like, based on the breed standard. The breed standard is the written formal description of the "perfect" Chihuahua. The standard is what breeders adhere to when trying to breed the ideal Chihuahua, and is also the model used by judges to select the dog in the show ring who best conforms to the ideal.

SIZE

The first noticeable physical characteristic of a Chihuahua is his tiny size. They are the smallest breed of dog in the world. Chis don't have a height limit, but their weight is restricted to 6 pounds (3 kg) and under. There are variations within this weight limit but most responsible breeders try to keep their breeding mothers to the uppermost size limit, hoping to reduce problems with birthing puppies. The males can be quite a bit smaller.

PUPPY POINTER

Even Chihuahua puppies have the typical Chihuahua attitude. Loni Osborne's Chihuahua puppy Suzie wasn't aware or didn't care that Loni's Standard Poodle was a big dog. When she brought Suzie home from the breeder, this tiny puppy walked up to him and barked into his mug—letting him know that she was the new *big* dog in town.

The Chihuahua is small but should be sturdy; the breed should never appear weedy or slender in build (like the Italian Greyhound). They are little dogs of substance and bone and should not appear frail. When you pick up a Chi, he should feel heavier than you would think. While he's not a bulky weight-lifter type of dog, he should be more solid than insubstantial. This is an important point—especially with unethical backyard breeders and puppy mills turning out poorly sized dogs. Well-bred Chihuahuas are shaped similar to a sturdy robust pony—not a lanky, leggy racehorse.

How Small Is Too Small?

Recently, "deer-type" and "teacup" Chihuahuas have become more prevalent. Deer-type Chihuahuas have fragile, thin legs and are lanky-looking. They look more deer-like than the correct sturdier build the standard calls for. Deer-type Chis do not conform to the standard, therefore they are not the correct type of body form. They should not be advertised by a breeder as "special" in order to bring in more money. Neither should "teacup" Chihuahuas, as this is a term that unscrupulous breeders have labeled puppies who are far below the proper weight and size. Deliberately breeding for the smallest of the small is risky because too-tiny dogs may come with accompanying health problems.

BODY

The Chihuahua body should be *off square*, so they are slightly longer than tall. Male Chis can be less than long in the body because they don't have the job of carrying puppies. There should be no hint of dwarfism. Chihuahuas have a good depth of chest and should not be thin and lanky, leggy, or slight.

HEAD

The head of the Chihuahua is *apple-domed*. The Chihuahua Club of America (CCA)'s Illustrated Standard compares the Chi's head to that of a "cooking apple" with a domed width between the ears. The roundness of the skull does not mean his cheeks are puffy, but rather they should be flat.

The skull is extremely rounded in appearance, with or without a *molera* (the soft spot on the Chihuahua's skull similar to a human baby). Unlike most other toy breeds, this molera is normal in Chihuahuas and is not a problem. Not every Chihuahua has this distinctive molera—it used to be required in the breed in 1923, but these days they come with or without the soft spot. Chis with a molera must be handled with care, and extra protection is needed for these dogs.

Stop

The Chi should have a well-defined *stop*, which is the area just above the eyes where the skull comes down to the muzzle. This angle ideally is about 90 degrees, which is considered deep. The stop is emphasized in the Standard because without it there would be no distinctive Chihuahua head.

Muzzle

There should be no downward or upward slope to the muzzle as seen from the side. The muzzle of the Chi is supposed to be reasonably short, and narrows from the jaw to the nose.

Nose

The Chi should not have a needle nose, nor the opposite extreme, a coarse, blunted nose. Chihuahuas have black, pink, or partially pigmented or multicolored noses. The nose can also be the same color as the dog's body, which is called self-colored.

Ears

The Chihuahua's ears are quite essential to the breed and go a long way to expressing the ideal look. The ears should be large and erect, held more upright

The Chihuahua has large eyes that are set wide apart.

when he's alert, and they should look like bat wings. Broken down ears that cannot be held upright are not ideal.

Expression
Aficionados of the breed say the Chihuahua has a saucy expression. A sullen expression is not desirable.

Eyes
His eyes are round but not protruding, and a lustrous dark or ruby color. Light-colored eyes are acceptable in blonde dogs. The eyes should be large and wide apart. You should be able to see the liveliness dancing in those eyes.

Bite
The Chi's bite (*dentition*) is important because a distorted jaw or teeth is not healthy for any dog, but especially for the Chihuahua, who can have dental problems throughout his life. Chis don't require a powerful bite like some of the working breeds or terriers because this is not a breed who hunts or needs a stronger bite.

The best bite is the *scissors* or *level* bite. With the scissors bite, the teeth of the upper jaw slightly cover the bottom incisors. With a level bite, the teeth meet edge to edge with no overlap. Minor bite imperfections are okay, but an extremely overshot or undershot jaw can contribute to problems with eating. His lips should not sag but be tight, and he should keep his tongue in his mouth when it's closed. An incorrect bite in a dog can contribute to the tongue hanging out of the dog's mouth. (If you've ever seen the Ugliest Dog Contest, you know what this means!)

TAIL
The tail is the finishing touch and is carried over the back in a loose semi-circular fashion called a *sickle*, never tucked between the legs or flat against the back. The tail is slightly thicker in the middle and tapers to a point.

MOVEMENT
The Chi is a swift and smoothly moving dog whose movement is compared to many working breeds that must move smoothly and effortlessly in order to do their job.

COAT

The breed comes in two coat types, the *smooth coat* and the *long coat*. However, aside from the difference in coat lengths, the two body types are the same. According to the breed standard, the structure considered ideal for the smooth coat is the same for the long coat.

Smooth coats are the most widely known variety. Their coats are soft, close lying, and glossy. They should have a slightly standoff of hair on the neck, which is called the *ruff*. Long coats are flat or slightly curly and have feathering or long hair on the legs, tail, and feet. They should have fringing on their ears and a plumed tail. Long coats have an undercoat and a ruff on the neck.

Chihuahua breeder Micki Giroux says, "Long coats are believed to be a little more laid-back with a softer disposition than their siblings with smooth coats."

COLOR

The acceptable colors for Chihuahuas are almost limitless. There is no discrimination in coat color—they can be any color, including brindle, red, fawn, black and tan, tri-color, or splashed "like a pinto horse" as one breeder described it. Not every breeder agrees with the acceptance of rare colors, but the standard does allow for almost any color.

Rare Colors Controversy

Michelle "Micki" Giroux, responsible breeder and Chihuahua expert says, "Rare colors are due to more recessive genes. These colors are usually associated with more health problems. But the 'new thing' is the merle-colored Chis; however, the old timers don't like them. Chihuahuas have so many health problems—why add more with merle blindness, hearing, and deformation problems? We don't want to bring more health issues into the breed. Other countries have banned [the merle color] . . . however it's a big fight right now in the U.S."

Chihuahuas come in two coat types, smooth and long.

TEMPERAMENT

Would you be surprised to learn that the miniscule Chihuahua is a tough dog, and the written standard says they are "terrier-like"? If you know anything about terriers, you know that means all attitude and tenacity. Chihuahuas are not just pretty faces, and their long history proves their staying power and toughness. Their ancestors who lived in mountainous or desert regions had to be hardy survivors.

When Chis are shown in the conformation ring, their temperaments can be more accurately judged when the dogs are on the ground. Standing on the ground in the show ring, they should be up on their toes and convey the alert posture that's typical of terriers. Many admirers of the breed say Chihuahuas don't know their own size and consider themselves imposing.

However, no characteristic should be extreme or over-exaggerated. The Chihuahua should express the overall impression of balance.

Good Breeding

The Chihuahua was once known as a shivering hand-biter with his tail tucked between his legs. However, serious breeders have worked hard to breed any of those undesirable characteristics out of their bloodlines. Today's Chihuahua is an alert breed but never nervous. Responsible breeders have worked hard at repairing the breed's negative reputation by creating a Chihuahua who is confident but not aggressive.

LIVING WITH A CHIHUAHUA

Getting a Chihuahua is like having an infant around for the 12 to 18 years or so that they live with you. You have to be careful of their safety all their lives, just like with an infant. In fact, if you enjoyed having a human baby, you will most likely love taking care of a Chihuahua.

Because of their small size, they can be with you practically everywhere you go. They are fairly low in the upkeep department—they don't require a lot of grooming, they eat very little, they don't need much exercise, and they are cheap to keep. And they live long healthy lives. They make wonderful pets for the elderly and the homebody.

PERSONALITY

Chihuahuas are a charming blend of attitude and affection.

Affection

The Chi is recognized as a companion par excellence. Chis are extremely devoted to their owners—bordering on person worship. They often pick out a person in the family who they "own" and take the protection of this person unusually seriously! They'll give absolute devotion to "their" person.

Chihuahuas are lively and constantly seek attention from their favorite people. These dogs will entertain you for many years with their energy and enthusiasm. Be prepared to devote a lot of time and affection to your Chi—he'll demand it. If you want your companion to be a "Velcro-dog" who sticks by your side, then you won't go wrong with a Chihuahua.

Attitude

Chis are confident, and they carry themselves with a haughty air. They can be slightly conceited and march around with an air of importance. Experts say the Chi is Napoleon in a dog suit, so he really does consider himself an important figure. This is a breed known for its fearlessness, which can be to its detriment.

However, Chihuahua personalities can range from retiring and mellow to bold and brassy. There are many Chihuahuas who are high-strung and shy, but that type of dog is usually a product of little or no socialization and poor breeding. Good breeders strive to produce dogs with desirable Chihuahua characteristics.

The rule is no timidity or extreme aggressiveness is allowed in the registry. However, Chihuahuas are allowed to be wary of strangers. They can be aloof with new people, but they should not be shy or panicked (e.g., hiding in corners or running for cover). And with some acquainting time, they should allow new people into their life.

They will stand their ground and own it, but should not bite. They are not the type of personality to run up to visitors and jump into the lap and lavish kisses on a stranger's

Chi's don't seem to be aware of their own size—they always see themselves as "top dog"!

Chihuahuas can do well with older children who understand how to handle a small dog.

face. This standoffishness gives them their own kind of charm.

COMPANIONABILITY

Chihuahuas are very playful and are generally pleasant to live with.

With Children

Because of the breed's size, they don't do well with young children, and even if the child is taught to be gentle, interactions should always be supervised. Children can unintentionally hurt a little dog. Chihuahuas do best with older children whose impulses are better under control and who can understand the concept of not hurting the animal.

Chihuahuas are protective of their own safety, so he can (rightly) be nippy if harshly treated. They do require socialization with older children who are taught how to handle them gently. They can hold a grudge, and if hurt by a young child, they can be nasty and intolerant—and no one wants that.

If you have young children, wait to get your Chihuahua until the kids are a bit older and can understand what could happen to a Chi who gets handled roughly (however unintentional it may be). If you already own a Chi with small children, *always supervise their interactions*.

With Other Pets

Although it's a controversial topic in the fancy, some Chihuahua owners claim that the breed is "snobby" and dislikes other breeds—but they do enjoy the company of their own kind. Owners claim that two Chihuahuas are better than one because they can keep each other company when you aren't available. They are often called a clannish breed.

However, if raised with other animals who treat the dogs with care, many owners have had success with Chihuahuas getting along with other breeds of

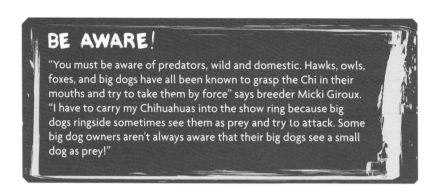

BE AWARE!

"You must be aware of predators, wild and domestic. Hawks, owls, foxes, and big dogs have all been known to grasp the Chi in their mouths and try to take them by force" says breeder Micki Giroux. "I have to carry my Chihuahuas into the show ring because big dogs ringside sometimes see them as prey and try to attack. Some big dog owners aren't always aware that their big dogs see a small dog as prey!"

dogs. They can get along with big dogs also, if the rule of gentleness is observed by the bigger dog. Even so, breeder Micki says she never recommends that Chihuahuas are left unsupervised with a big dog.

Chis generally live with cats peacefully if the cats are gentle with the Chihuahua.

ENVIRONMENT

Chis can live anywhere. They do fine in the city, the suburbs, or the country. As long as they are protected from harsh weather and predators and live indoors with you, they can flourish.

It may seem obvious, but it's worth noting: *Chihuahuas are not outside dogs.* They have to live indoors to survive. Their tiny frames can't handle the cold, and they must be guarded from danger. Chis generally have thinner coats than dogs like Siberian Huskies who were bred to work outside. If you live in a cold climate, they may not want to go outside even with a warm coat on. They can shiver and be miserable in the cold and wet, because they are so small and lose body heat rapidly.

Chihuahuas can be excessive barkers, especially if not properly raised and socialized as puppies. This may be due to feeling threatened because everything is so much larger than they are. Or, it may be because they see themselves as guardians of their home and their people. Chihuahuas may bark if bored or lonely, and some Chis with separation anxiety will bark unduly. Barking can be a nuisance if you live in an apartment or a home that's close to the neighbors.

EXERCISE REQUIREMENTS

Chis have low exercise requirements. A daily walk around a short block is sufficient, and in a pinch many owners find they can exercise their dogs by playing and running around the house. But don't rely too much on indoor exercise. Every dog deserves an outdoor walk with his owner. Even if it's a very short walk, it does wonders for a Chihuahua's mental attitude and physical fitness.

GROOMING

For a short-coated Chihuahua, grooming is minimal because of his short coat and the small size of the dog. If you are showing a short-coated Chi, grooming requires more time, however his grooming needs are still considered minor. A long-coated Chihuahua requires a touch more time, but then the grooming needs are still negligible compared to many other dog breeds.

HEALTH

Chihuahuas are generally healthy dogs. However, due to his tiny body, he can have health issues like hypoglycemia, luxating patellas, and dental problems. Collapsing trachea is another health issue that's considered more common in toy dogs, including the Chihuahua. It's theorized by some experts that since Chihuahuas are so close to the ground, they may be at more risk to toxins because they are exposed to cleaning substances on floors or chemically treated grass.

Chis have low exercise requirements, but they still love a fun outdoor walk with their owners.

TRAINABILITY

Chihuahuas can be a challenge to train, so their trainability is on the low end of the spectrum. They are bred to be self-confident dogs with an enormous attitude that you wouldn't expect from such a teeny dog. Chis are bred to stand their ground despite their small frame. They are expected to be "saucy" and "filled up with themselves," which can translate into "hard to train." However, with persistence and dedication on the part of the owner, they can be trained quite well. Just because they may be harder to train than other breeds doesn't mean they aren't intelligent. In fact, it's his intelligence that can make training more challenging than with other breeds who have the desire to please. He often considers his own judgment to be better than yours and will make you work hard to convince him to do it your way.

THE JITTERS

The Chihuahua can get the "jitters," which appears as quivering or shivering. It can stem from nervous unreleased energy or from being cold. If you constantly carry your dog around, he may never learn to feel comfortable on his own four feet. Let him walk on the ground in situations that you know are not dangerous.

Chihuahuas tend to get along with other Chihuahuas.

Lisa Garrison's Chihuahuas hate cold weather. She says, "My Chihuahuas prefer to be indoors, with short jaunts outside if the weather is warm, and when it's brisk outside they want a coat—if they absolutely have to be outdoors. They are like me in that respect, I won't usually go outside when it's chilly, even with a coat! I just don't want to . . . you have to pry my dogs outside even when it's 65°F (18°C)!"

When you carry your Chihuahua and he shivers, it's often because he needs to blow excess energy. If your Chi can't run around to release energy, then it is natural that the trembles will start.

PAMPERING

Chis require plenty of pampering—at least according to owners. "Suzie needs to be lifted into and out of her favorite places, even if it's accessible to her. They want you to do certain things for them to prove that you prize them," says Chi owner Loni Osborne. "I bought a special clothes basket for Suzie that I fill with warm clothes straight from the dryer every day for her to lie in until they cool. I don't wash every day, but I have to run some items through the dry cycle just for her every morning. If I miss a day, she sulks and makes me feel quite guilty." Loni continues, "I place the basket on top of an antique trunk in my computer room so the other dogs don't bother her. She waits for me to lift her out of the basket when she's decided she's done. She doesn't whine or bark to get my attention. She just stands up and stares at me. I picture a bubble over her head (like in the old cartoons) with 'Why aren't you giving me your 100% attention all the time?' encapsulated above her."

SUPPLIES FOR YOUR CHIHUAHUA

The hand-painted banner across the living room reads "Welcome Home Chi-Chi." You set little Chi-Chi on the floor, and he looks around his new digs and thinks "What the … where's my stuff?" There's no food or water dish, and he has no bed, not even a collar and leash to take him outside. He's too little to go out alone and crossing his legs doesn't even enter his little baby head … and he's hungry … now!

You forgot to go out and buy dog supplies before you brought Chi-Chi home and now you have to load him back up in the car and head out again. You can't leave him home alone after that stressful drive away from his littermates and everything he's ever known and everyone he holds dear—he'd never forgive you!

Sound exaggerated? Generally, bringing a puppy or new dog home will be dramatic for you both, but hopefully not traumatic. It's best to bring a new dog into a dog-savvy home that's not devoid of everything he needs and wants. So, pull out some paper and a pencil and start a list of the dog supplies you'll need. Here are some items that are necessities to care for your new Chihuahua, and some that are just plain nice to have on hand.

BEDS

If you have a puppy, until he grows out of his chewing stage and is housetrained, you will want an inexpensive and washable pet bed. Don't buy the most expensive bed they sell (at least in the baby months). Puppies can be like baby sharks: They want to put everything in their mouths. There will be time for posh, cute things as time goes by.

After the housetraining phase is over, the options for beds are unlimited in style and price. From basic unadorned pads, to designer beds, to miniature canopy beds complete with mattresses, let your budget and your Chi's comfort be your guide. If your floors are hard and your dog follows you throughout the house, consider purchasing a few beds that can be left in different rooms throughout the house. Remember that Chis get chilled easily, so here are a few excellent options:

- Beds with heating elements inside that you can turn on or off. Some have thermostats so that you can adjust the temperature with the seasons. (Chi's seem to adore these types of beds!)
- Small pet-safe heating elements that can be inserted into a zippered bed can be found in pet supply stores.
- Microwaveable hard discs made expressly for pet beds can be warmed and inserted under or into a bed. After six minutes in the microwave, they will stay warm for hours. These are often inexpensive and can be reused for years. You can also purchase a cover for these discs to maintain the heat and protect your Chi's skin.

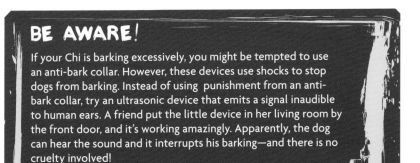

- Dog beds that the dog can crawl into are a lovely way for your Chi to get warm and hide away if he wants to. They look like a large pocket and they are fleecy and warm.

Be careful—some of these items can get hot, so test the temperature on yourself and make sure to cover the warming elements so you don't burn your Chi's sensitive skin.

CARRIER

Carriers come in handy when you take your dog on outings, to visit the veterinarian, and traveling with you. Carrying a Chi in your purse is dangerous and not very comfortable for the dog. Carriers designed specifically for dogs have non-collapsible frames and padded bottoms.

Carriers come in a variety of designs and fabrics. The one you choose will be determined by whether or not your Chi will ever be flying with you. If you'll be jet-setting together, you'll need an airline-approved carrier. It's the safest way to go for your Chihuahua's comfort and security.

To choose the best small dog carrier ask yourself:

- Is there enough room for your Chihuahua to move around a bit? Can your dog stand up and turn around inside the carrier?
- Is the carrier well ventilated? He needs air circulation inside, so ventilated sides with roll-up panels are a good option.
- Is the carrier padded and comfortable?
- Is it made of material that you can clean off, or is it washable?
- Will it fit on your car seat with a way that allows you to attach it to the seat, or does it come with an attachment to fasten it to the seat belt?
- Is it airline approved? The airlines have strict regulations for carriers that will fit under your seat.

- Is it durable?
- Is there a pocket or two to stash a few things like extra food or health papers?

Carriers are often used instead of crates for travel because they are lighter and more portable than a crate—plus, crates aren't allowed as carry-ons on flights, but carriers are. Both a crate and a carrier have their place in your dog's life.

COLLAR/HARNESS AND LEASH

Purchase a collar and have your pup start wearing it right away. Leather, nylon, or cotton collars are all good choices for the Chihuahua, as long as they are supple, soft, and lightweight. Collars should be soft and non-chafing; either a buckle or break-away type collar is fine. Buy a collar that's not so large that it slips off—it should fit snugly, but you should be able to get a finger between the collar and the dog's neck. Check the kitty section for collars that are small enough to fit your Chihuahua. Choke chains are not recommended because they can damage your Chi's neck.

Collars should be used to hang ID tags on, but you should never tie up or walk a Chihuahua in his collar because a collar can easily damage his trachea—use a harness instead. Harnesses are a recommended option for your Chihuahua because they are not hard on your dog's trachea. Collars can dig into his small

A light, well-fitted collar or harness is a good choice for your Chihuahua.

neck and cause choking and even tracheal collapse. Make sure the harness you buy is fitted to avoid choking. Harnesses are made of mesh, fabric, or nylon and can be lined with sheepskin-like fabrics. Some harnesses are ingenuously designed to be used as a seatbelt in your car, too.

Most Chi owners prefer a 4 to 6 foot (1 to 2 m) leash made out of nylon or narrow diameter leather. If you are tall, you may need a longer leash that allows your dog to comfortably walk. Just be sure the clip on the leash is not the heavy type used for large dogs. Buy a lighter clip and light leash, which will put less pressure on your Chi's neck. Retractable leads are also available and can be used to give your dog more range when on a walk; some extend up to 26 feet (8 m) long. However, the shorter retractable leads are safer and lighter for the Chi.

CRATE

Crate training your dog can set him up for success the rest of his life. The crate will be his sanctuary—a sort of plush doggy den—and a valuable training tool. It will make housetraining easier, and if you are going to travel with your Chihuahua a crate may be necessary. When your puppy goes to visit the vet for neutering or spaying, he or she will be accustomed to being confined in a crate and it will be less traumatic for your little one. Plus, getting your dog conditioned to a crate will go a long way toward protecting him against separation anxiety. Even if you don't plan on having your Chihuahua sleep in a crate every night, you are well advised to crate train him.

Get a small-sized crate for your Chihuahua. Chihuahuas don't need a giant crate; get one that your puppy fits into with a few extra inches (cm) of room to grow into. A crate that's closer to his own size will make him feel secure. Think of it this way, if you were lost in the vast wilderness, wouldn't you like a tent to sleep in rather than out in the open, which would only make you feel vulnerable? It's similar to a tiny pup new to your home—when things get overwhelming, a crate will give him a place to take his own time-out. *Please note that the crate should not be used as a form of punishment or to confine him for hours on end.*

Ideally, an airline-approved fiberglass or plastic-sided crate or a wire crate is best. The fiberglass crates make a bedroom that's draft free for a Chi and that's an important consideration. Soft-sided crates are available but won't stand up to chewing and potty messes.

You can make your dog's crate comfy by using old towels or blankets, or buy a pad that's washable until your pup is housetrained. Don't use potty pads to have your Chihuahua sleep on—they are treated with a scent to encourage a puppy to wee, and you don't want to promote elimination in his crate.

EXERCISE PEN

Exercise pens (ex-pens) are portable pens consisting of panels made of epoxy-coated wire. The interlocking panels can be configured into different arrangements either outside or in indoor areas. They don't have tops, but are tall enough to keep puppies in and short enough that you can reach in and retrieve your Chihuahua.

Ex-pens are convenient for travel and can be used outside if you don't have a fence—just stake them into the ground and secure a sunshade to the top. If you do use them outside, you'll still need to supervise your Chihuahua, as he could still be in danger from roaming dogs who might knock over the ex-pen or reach in and grab your small dog.

Indoors, ex-pens can be used to confine puppies when they are being housetrained. Put a bed at one end of the pen and pee pads or newspaper on the other end when you're not there to supervise. Dogs don't like to relieve themselves where they sleep, so this will help your pup to learn to "hold it."

FOOD AND WATER BOWLS

Your Chihuahua will need food and water bowls. Stainless steel or ceramic bowls are safe and long-lasting, and they can be sterilized in a dishwasher or washed in your sink. These types of high-quality bowls are better for your Chihuahua than ones made of plastic. Remember, puppies chew and the cheap plastic bowls can literally be eaten, and they are often made of products that don't belong in any dog's tummy.

Bowls should be low sided and wide bottomed so they can't be tipped over easily, and not so large that they become a swimming pool.

FOOD CONTAINERS

Airtight pet food containers are a good investment for storing your Chihuahua's dog food. They keep food fresh and rodents out.

GATES

Indoor gates can be helpful when you are too busy to watch your puppy but want him to have a little room to play. These gates are used to partition off a room, and they may save your sanity—especially while your Chihuahua is a baby. You can find gates made of metal, plastic, or wood. Some have gates that swing out, and some have locking mechanisms to keep your Chihuahua from accidently opening them. Many are slatted, and some have clear see-through panels. Be careful of the type you get because pups will often chew on them, and their teeth may get caught in tiny openings or mesh.

GROOMING SUPPLIES

Necessary grooming items include brushes; soft-bristle brushes are a good choice for smooth coats, and a metal fine tooth comb and small pin brush are good investments for long coats. You will need either a nail grinder or nail cutters—cat nail clippers work well for the Chihuahua's small paws. Other essential items include ear cleaning solution, mild dog shampoo, and styptic powder or pads.

A toothbrush and dental gel or doggy toothpaste are also necessary supplies

You'll have to invest in a few grooming supplies.

Keep ID tags attached to your Chi's collar.

for your Chihuahua. Chihuahuas have small mouths, and this causes their teeth to crowd together, which in turn causes dental problems. So, brushing their teeth is essential. Fingertip toothbrushes are small and soft enough for puppy mouths and even into adulthood. Always buy dog toothpaste—it is flavored especially for dogs and is safe for them to swallow.

Some optional items you might want to consider are a handheld pet hair dryer and a caddy or tote to keep all of your grooming supplies together. A grooming table made for little dogs can be a convenient item. Grooming supply stores sell tables that fold up to store out of the way. If you don't want to go to the expense of a designated grooming table, you might want to buy a small rotating grooming table. These can be placed on the ground or on any flat surface, like your kitchen table. These non-slip tables have an arm and loop that will hold your Chi still. The diameter is generally 18 to 27 inches (46 to 67 cm), and the top rotates so you can sit down and move the top of the table around while you groom.

IDENTIFICATION

Your best chance of getting your Chihuahua back if he ever gets lost is to have some type of identification on him. ID tags on a collar or a microchip implanted under the skin are the two best ways. Tags are a good way to identify your dog;

they are easy to find and reasonably priced. Some owners find that the tags can be ungainly for Chihuahuas and choose not to leave a collar on their dogs when indoors. However, one little slip and your Chi-Chi could be out the door with no way to ID him. Plus, tags can fall off or become illegible with wear, so it's best to also have a more permanent means of identification.

Microchipping is a permanent way to ID your Chihuahua. A microchip is a tiny transponder, about the size of a grain of rice, that is implanted under your dog's skin. Each chip has its own number, and when a reader is passed over that area on your dog, the number can be read. A microchip needs to be registered with a recovery service, which stores your contact information so your dog can find his way back to you. Microchips are recommended by vets and rescue organizations. Some microchips come with ID tags that list the toll-free phone number to the chip registry.

Tattoos located on the inside of a dog's thigh were once the primary method of permanent identification, but are no longer as common. The problem with tattoos is deciding what number to use. The other issue with a small dog like the Chi is that the inside thigh area is too tiny to tattoo much information. However,

Your Chi will get chilled easily, and coats and sweaters are necessary even if you live in a temperate climate.

tattoos are still used by some people, and a tattoo will stay with your pup for life. If you tattoo your Chi, have it done during the spay or neuter, when your pup is already anesthetized.

SWEATERS AND COATS

The Chihuahua craves the sunshine and the warmth it provides. Toy dogs, and Chihuahuas in particular, can't stand the cold because they lose body heat rapidly. Your Chi will get chilled easily, and coats and sweaters are necessary even if you live in a temperate climate. Dog apparel comes in a vast variety or colors and styles. You can even find "couture" fashions in specialty stores and online. Tee-shirts, sweaters, jackets, and rainwear are all available. Your Chi doesn't need to be in the latest trends, but a sweater and a warm coat are good investments that are worth the price.

TOYS

Your Chi will think toys are a necessity and so should you. Your dog needs toys to provide stimulation and further develop the bond between you two. Toys are also a good way to introduce training. You can use them as a way to start teaching your Chi basic commands like *come* and *drop it*.

Make sure the toys you buy are safe, and if you have a puppy, find toys made specifically for that age. There should be no small parts that can be chewed off and swallowed. Squeakers in toys can be torn out and swallowed, so always supervise your dog and pick up stuffing and squeakers when your Chi is finished playing. Most toys and chews come with disclaimers that state the items should be monitored and taken away if the dog chews off pieces and starts to eat them.

A great variety of toys are available, so have fun. Interactive toys can provide some mental stimulation for your Chi. These toys require the dog to use his brainpower to get a treat that's often hidden inside a puzzle toy or a hollow rubber chew.

Chew toys are essential. Buy one that is not so large it won't fit in his mouth and not so hard that it will chip or break teeth. Hard rubber chews and other shapes are a good option and are hard to break apart. You can stuff rubber toys with peanut butter or soft cheese and freeze them to occupy your dog when he's bored.

Make sure to bring your Chihuahua along with you to the pet store to help you decide which toy he wants to take home.

WASTE MANAGEMENT

While your Chihuahua should be trained to go potty outside, occasionally you may be detained at work or out longer than anticipated. You may want to give your Chi the option of going in a litter box. Dog litter boxes are available at dog supply stores and are a good option for those times when your Chi may need to potty indoors.

Indoor dog potties are also available. They consist of a rectangular floor tray with a turf-covered mat that fits inside. The liquid seeps through the turf and collects in the tray for disposal. These potties use either real or synthetic grass, so your Chi will feel more like he's answering the call of nature out in nature!

Pee pads are another option during the housetraining period or if you need to leave your Chi for longer than he can hold it. The pads are made of layers of material that absorb liquid waste, and the bottom layer protects the floor underneath the pad. Most dogs will return to an area that carries a faint whiff of urine, so pee pads contain a scent that attracts dogs to the pads to do their business.

THE SKY'S THE LIMIT!

Fancy pooper-scoopers, doggy cabanas, dog pools and cooling mats, raised beds, doggy couches, orthopedic pads, mattresses, strollers, and a million more doggy things that I can't begin to describe here—they're all available for your Chihuahua! You'll have the pleasure of getting out to the pet supply stores to discover them all for yourself. Be assured that if you can think of something that you need, it's out there.

FEEDING YOUR CHIHUAHUA

You could get a Ph.D. in animal nutrition and still be baffled by all the variety in dog foods offered today. Get online and read any of the available information about feeding your dog, and you'll quickly find out that nobody agrees completely on feeding our canine friends. It seems like every time we hear a great new theory on what is best for our dogs, it ends up disputed by scientific studies. So, what's a new owner to do? This chapter can help you wade through the abundance of information out there.

NUTRITION AND YOUR CHIHUAHUA

Nutrition is especially important when it comes to Chihuahuas. Their stomachs are so small they can't take in a lot of food, so when it comes to diet there's less margin for error than with big dogs. With Chihuahuas, every bite of food has to be high quality.

Even though they have small stomachs, pound for pound, Chihuahuas actually need *more* food than larger dogs. Diminutive Chis have power-driven metabolisms, and the energy they get from food can rapidly be used up. Plus, the Chihuahua dissipates heat more rapidly than some other breeds, which also uses up energy.

The food a Chihuahua gets throughout his life can impact his health and can determine his quality of life. If he doesn't get the best food, he may suffer from dental diseases and other illnesses. A poor diet may even influence his relationship with you—an undernourished dog can be cranky and lethargic, and that's not a Chihuahua who's fun to be with.

BASIC NUTRITION

Dogs' nutritional needs vary, even within the same breed. It can be confusing trying to figure it all out. But there are basic nutrients that every dog needs.

WATER

Water isn't often thought of as a nutrient, but it's essential to life. It is just as important as the food you feed your dog. Good hydration helps promote the normal functions of the body systems. Water is needed to move nutrients

The food a Chihuahua gets throughout his life can impact his health.

Vitamins and minerals help the immune system function properly.

through your Chi's body and to remove waste through urination.

Your Chihuahua needs unrestricted access to clean, fresh water. Clean your dog's water bowl frequently to keep it sanitary, and refill it with fresh water daily or more often if needed. Just as it's ideal to monitor your dog's food intake, you should have a general idea about how much your dog drinks on a daily basis. A dog who isn't drinking enough or stops drinking can end up in trouble.

PROTEIN

Protein is essential for all life stages of your Chihuahua. Proteins serve as building blocks for the body. They help repair tissues, bones, muscles, and produce enzymes and antibodies. Sources for protein can come from plants or animals. Common proteins found in dog food include beef, chicken, lamb, fish, and other meats, as well as dairy and eggs. The ingredient list will give you an indicator of the type and quality of protein contained in a food.

FAT

Fat plays many roles in your Chihuahua's body. Fat is required for energy and to help support internal organs, the nervous system, and coat health. Chihuahuas need fat to maintain their core body temperature when they become chilled.

Fat increases the taste and palatability of your dog's food—but it also increases the calorie count.

The right kinds of fat are important for dog nutrition. Essential fatty acids (omega-3 and omega-6) are often included in some commercial foods, usually in the form of fish oil. These fats may improve brain function and contribute to a healthy skin and coat. Beef tallow and lamb are very low in essential fatty acids, so they should not make up a large part of your dog's food.

CARBOHYDRATES

Carbohydrates are needed to produce energy in the body. They come in several forms, including starches found in plant products like potato and grains. Complex starches are good because they are a longer-lasting energy source. Simple carbs and sugars are not preferred for dog food because (just like in our diet) they contain empty calories with no nutritional value. Fiber is another carbohydrate that comes from indigestible cellulose and is needed for normal digestion. It helps to keep your Chihuahua fit and trim by making him feel full and satisfied.

MINERALS AND VITAMINS

Minerals and vitamins are necessary for bone growth, healing, nerve and muscle function, fluid balance, and overall metabolism. They also help the immune system function properly, which helps fight off illnesses. Both minerals and vitamins are needed in the right balance and specific ratios. Too much of certain minerals and vitamins can cause just as many health problems as deficiencies can.

COMMERCIAL DOG FOOD

It used to be that dog owner's didn't have much of a choice when it came to dog food—cheap dry kibble or canned dog food were about it. Today, pet owners are demanding quality ingredients, more natural ingredients, and less by-products and additives. Some dog foods are specialized for performance, while others are available by prescription. Whether you feed a special diet or a traditional dog food you still need to tailor what you feed to your Chihuahua's needs. Your Chi's age, size, health, and activity level all determine how much and what kind of food you feed your dog.

DRY (KIBBLE)

Many people find dry dog food (also called kibble) the most convenient type of food. Dry foods are generally less expensive by weight than wet (canned) or semi-moist foods. Dry foods don't go rancid as quickly as wet and are more nutritionally dense because they don't have the high moisture content of canned and semi-moist foods. Dry food has about three and a half times more calorie density than canned food.

The nutritional value of kibble varies widely. Dry food can contain more filler, like wheat or corn. If you choose to feed kibble, make sure you buy a brand made with quality ingredients.

You don't need to feed dry kibble dry. Soaking the dry food with water and mixing in a small amount of canned dog food can make it more appetizing for your Chihuahua. However, when you feed a mixture of dry and canned dog food, keep in mind the total caloric intake that the combination provides.

Dry food is available in different shapes and sizes. Be sure to get the smaller size for your Chihuahua.

SEMI-MOIST

Semi-moist dog food is convenient because it often comes in easy-to-open packets and has a long shelf life. However, you might notice a chemical odor

when you first open this kind of dog food—that's because of the all the additives. Plus, semi-moist dog food has more sugar than kibble or wet food. Semi-moist foods are probably not the best choice for a healthy diet for your Chihuahua.

WET (CANNED)

Some people prefer to feed their dogs wet or canned dog food. The food is sterilized after being canned so it's safe. Many Chihuahuas prefer the taste of canned food and will gobble it up. Wet food makes a good supplement to dry, and it can perk up the appetite if needed. Canned food is often higher in protein or fat, but you must feed more of it than dry. Wet food is more expensive to feed, but with your Chihuahua's tiny belly it shouldn't break the bank.

Many Chihuahuas prefer the taste of canned food.

A 6-month-old Chihuahua didn't like the puppy food his owner had purchased for him—he refused to eat it. The owner was disappointed because it was the best-quality food she could find in her area. As a last resort, she got down on the floor and acted like she was eating the food out of his bowl. Now her Chi can't get enough of his chow!

DOG FOOD LABELS

In the United States, the Association of American Feed Control Officials (AAFCO) regulates the quality and safety of pet food. AAFCO sets the standards on food labels, which must contain a guaranteed analysis and a nutritional adequacy statement. Labels that state that the foods are "complete and balanced" must meet the standards that AAFCO puts in place.

By law, ingredients are listed in descending order by weight. One way to find a good dog food is to be sure the food uses more meat than grains or soy as protein sources. Dogs can more easily digest higher-quality proteins derived from meat rather than other sources. High-quality dog foods have meats at the top of the list by weight.

However, keep in mind that some manufacturers play a "labeling game" with the ingredients by listing separately the same ingredient in a different form. It's called "splitting," and is a widely used practice of dividing up the less desirable ingredients into different names in order to make it seem like there's not as much. For example, corn may be listed as the second ingredient on the label, but you may also notice corn gluten and corn bran or flour further down on the label. Splitting up the various forms of corn disguises the total amount in the dog food. You may even be looking at a food that is more grain than meat—even if meat is listed first.

Preservatives

Dog foods use synthetic and natural preservatives to keep food from spoiling. Synthetic preservatives include BHA, BHT, and ethoxyquin, which may increase the risk of canine cancer. Propyl gallate and propylene glycol are other synthetic preservatives, and little is known about their toxicity or safety. Dog owners, trainers, and breeders suspect these synthetics of causing health problems, including skin disorders, reproductive issues, and allergies. Even though these links are unproven, there is some evidence that long-term ingestion of some preservatives can be problematic. Also, dogs can be allergic to certain food additives or colors.

Natural preservatives are thought to be safer. Some dog food manufacturers are using vitamin C, vitamin E, and clove, rosemary, or other spices to preserve their dog foods. Dogs can be allergic to certain food additives or colors.

Terms

Some dog foods that are labeled as "premium" or "gourmet" can be marketing schemes. These claims have no official regulatory standing. They are not required to have any higher quality ingredients or nutritional value other than any other complete or balanced dog food. "Natural" is another term often used on dog food packaging that has no official definition.

Serving Size

Beware of the serving size suggestion on dog food labels. While many owners follow the label's directions, if your Chi is not at his optimum weight, adjust the amount accordingly.

NON-COMMERICAL DIETS

Non-commercial diets run the range from home-cooked (cooking meals from scratch for your dog) to raw food (which consists of a balance of raw meaty bones and raw fruits and vegetables).

While it is possible for your Chihuahua to thrive on these types of diets, they are more difficult than opening a bag of dry kibble, and there is controversy in

A home-cooked diet may consist of cooked meat, vegetables, and certain supplements.

Dog Tale

Millie, a 7-pound (3-kg) Chihuahua, loved handouts from her owner's kitchen table. She ended up getting so fat that her owner not only put her on a diet, but they walk on a treadmill together. Millie didn't quite like it at first (a trait most humans can relate to), but now she's a pro!

the scientific community about feeding them. While proponents believe these diets are healthier for dogs, there are no scientific studies to prove it. Always check with your veterinarian or a canine nutritionist before settling on a home-cooked or raw diet. You can find animal nutritionists online through the American Holistic Veterinary Medical Association (AHVMA), or ask your vet for a referral

HOME-COOKED DIET

Home-cooked diets usually consist of cooked meat, vegetables, ground bone, taurine supplements, and other vitamin supplements specifically made for dogs. If you decide to prepare home-cooked dog food, you will need to commit the time it will take to researching, purchasing, and preparing it. Until you understand canine nutrition and your individual Chihuahua's needs, stick with prepared foods.

Some homemade diets are good for dogs with food allergies or other health issues because they generally have no preservatives or additives that can irritate a sensitive system, and they can be tailored to be free of any allergens that affect your individual Chihuahua.

RAW DIETS

A raw food diet consists of feeding a dog uncooked meats, organs, and edible bones instead of conventional commercial dog food. Raw dog food diet supporters believe that this is the ideal diet for dogs, because it mimics that of their wild ancestors. Opponents believe that the risk of feeding raw food is too high. For example, handling raw food increases the risks of food-borne illnesses and can carry parasites and other risks to the dog.

Plus, you'll have some additional concerns when it comes to feeding your Chihuahua. While big dogs can eat a variety of meats and bones safely, it's more difficult to feed a toy dog who can't eat the larger bones, and for safety reasons can't eat chicken bones or smaller bones.

Another problem is that it is difficult to balance a raw food diet correctly. If you feed raw food, be sure you check with a veterinary nutritionist about your recipe.

If you still want to go raw, but decide against formulating your own raw food recipe, you can buy raw food from various suppliers. Raw food sold in pet stores is safer than raw meats sold in grocery stores. The acceptable level of bacteria in meat meant for humans is actually higher because the meat is supposed to be cooked before consumption. The acceptable level of bacteria in raw foods produced for dogs is two percent or less because it is meant to be fed raw.

ALTERNATIVE COMMERICAL DOG FOODS

Because of the demand from customers for better nutrition for their pets, new types of dog food are being offered on the market that are different from established dog foods. They fall somewhere between traditional commercial food and homemade diets.

Examples include:

- **Fresh** or **Refrigerated**, in which the fresh ingredients are pasteurized. The foods are lightly cooked and then vacuum packaged. This type of food is vulnerable to spoilage so make sure to keep it refrigerated.
- **Frozen** or **Freeze-dried**, which comes in raw or cooked (though not processed) forms. By skipping the processing stage of traditional dog food, it's thought that there is less destruction of the nutrients. The products are then frozen or freeze-dried.
- **Dehydrated**, which also comes in raw and cooked types. This type looks very similar to dry dog food. Products are dried to reduce the moisture content so that bacterial growth is inhibited. Before serving this type of food, warm water is often added to produce gravy.

PUPPY/ADULT FOODS

Puppy food is a specially formulated diet that contains the extra nutrients and calories that growing pups need. Some experts feed their adult Chihuahuas puppy food throughout their lives, because they believe that, even as adults, Chis still need the extra nutrition.

Many breeders will include a small amount of puppy food to take home with your new puppy. Just ask the breeder what the brand and type of food it is, and if it's a high-quality food, you can continue to feed it.

WHEN TO FEED

You have two basic choices about when to feed your Chi—on a schedule (usually twice a day) or free feeding, which means leaving food out all day.

Many Chihuahua breeders prefer feeding on a scheduled basis, because this way they can monitor how much their dogs are eating during the day. Some breeders measure out the amount a dog should be eating in an entire day and divide it up into three or four scheduled feedings. However, feeding this way can be too restrictive for someone who's at work or can't be home at the scheduled times.

Some people prefer free feeding so their Chihuahuas can eat all day long, which ensures they are eating enough to stave off empty bellies and possible hypoglycemia. Hypoglycemia is a concern with toy dogs in general and particularly Chihuahuas, who are the smallest of the dog breeds.

If you decide to leave food out all the time, many breeders suggest that you wait until your Chi is an adult. Keep to a scheduled feeding plan when working on housetraining your puppy. It makes it easier to figure out when to take your puppy outside to do his business. And, you will become accustomed to your puppy's appetite and figure how much he will eat at each feeding.

OBESITY

Obesity is considered a huge health problem with many dogs in the United States (and not surprisingly with many American humans as well). Obesity is common in dogs who live a life of leisure with frequent overeating. And it is easy to overindulge your Chi—it can be hard to resist those big, lustrous, begging eyes. Plus, boredom from being indoors with little activity can cause a Chihuahua to want to eat more than is normal.

But don't let your Chihuahua's appetite be your guide to feeding him. Dogs are legendary for their desire to overeat. It may have something to do with their wild ancestors having to eat as much as they could in one sitting, because they may not have had the opportunity to eat again for some time. Plus, many owners start overfeeding their Chihuahuas because they fear hypoglycemia, which is a normal concern that breeder's emphasize when they send a puppy home. Instead of overfeeding to avoid this problem, a safer way is to take the total amount your Chi needs in one day, divide it into smaller meals, and feed throughout the day. You can ask your veterinarian to guide you.

Keep in mind that the stomach of a 4-pound (2-kg) animal is extremely undersized, and toy dogs don't need huge amounts of calories. A few extra pounds (kg) on a Chihuahua are akin to countless extra pounds (kg) on us, and carry

If you add treats to your dog's diet, take into account the extra calories.

many of the same health risks that overweight humans are warned about.

However, at times being overweight is not caused by overeating, but by health issues, including thyroid problems, Cushing's disease, and others. Get your Chi checked at your vet's office if he becomes obese.

How can you tell if your Chi is overweight? When looked at from above, a healthy dog should have a slight tuck in his waist behind the ribs. You should be able to feel his ribs under his skin and coat.

The best way to keep extra weight off your Chihuahua is the same way suggested for humans—exercise and the right amount and type of food. Always measure the food you put in your dog's bowl, and allow your overweight Chi a predetermined amount of time to eat it (generally a half an hour is plenty of time). When that time is up, take the bowl away.

TREATS

Treats are handy to use in training as a reward, but use nutritional sense with them. If you add treats to your dog's diet, take into account the extra calories, and subtract them from your dog's regular meals. If used in excess, dog treats can contribute to weight problems.

Lots of store-bought treats have artificial flavors and colors, so research them the way you would a commercial dog food. Look for nutritious treats without additives. Even though your Chi will be eating a small amount of treats in total, you still should avoid ones loaded with unhealthy things. Many commercial treats are too large to give at one time, so break them into tiny pieces and use those to reward your Chi. An alternative is to use a high-quality small dog kibble as a treat.

GROOMING YOUR CHIHUAHUA

et you thought when you got a Chihuahua that you'd get out of the brushing chore. That may have been one of the attractions of the breed. After all, how much grooming work could that tiny little character need? Whether you have a smooth or a long coat Chi, you still have to groom your Chihuahua if you want him to have a healthy skin and coat. However, from start to finish, grooming does not take much time—even for the long-coat Chihuahua. So, feel free to give yourself an internal congratulatory high-five for making the right choice for the breed with the smallest grooming needs.

GROOMING IS GOOD FOR HEALTH

Grooming is a wonderful way to bond with your pet. Chihuahuas like to be the center of attention, and grooming your dog provides him with your total undivided focus. Your Chihuahua will be soothed by your gentle brushing and the time you spend together. But grooming is not only a way to bond with your Chi—it is good for his health. Regular grooming is the best way to keep tabs on your Chi's health. Each time you go over your pet's body with your hands, feel for any changes since the last time you groomed him. Practiced regularly, you will learn to notice any differences in the dog's skin, coat, and overall appearance. New growths, warts, or lumps will be caught early. Find anything out of the ordinary during these checks, and you can put it on your list to ask your veterinarian about it.

One other great thing about grooming your Chi is that it's good for your health as well. Any time spent touching your pet lowers your blood pressure and makes you calmer.

GETTING USED TO GROOMING

When you bring your new Chi puppy home and he settles in, take some time every day to get him used to being touched. You can use this technique with an adult dog as well, but it may take extra time and patience if he's not accustomed to being handled or has ingrained bad habits to break. Put him on your lap while you watch TV and run your hands over his body. Handle his feet and toes, including holding on to each toe, so that the restraint won't scare him when you trim his nails. Massage his gums so dental care will be easy. Give your Chi pup lots of praise as he allows you to do these things. He will learn to love being touched, and it can be a great way to calm him when you need to. Conditioning the pup to handling will make grooming easier, and will make being handled by the veterinarian easier.

You should also get your Chi used to the tools you will be using on him. Let your Chihuahua get a good sniff of every tool first, and then praise him. Use them as you caress his body. Take your time and keep the mood light—don't get annoyed or scare him during this process.

YOUR CHI'S GROOMING SUPPLIES

Both long- and short-coated Chihuahuas will need the following grooming supplies:

- **Coat conditioner:** for long coats to detangle or condition the hair; for smooth coats to spray lightly to condition coat.
- **Cotton balls:** soak with ear cleaning solution to swab out ears.
- **Ear cleaning solution:** to clean out debris and wax from the ear.
- **Grinder or nail clippers (guillotine or scissors type):** if you want clippers, cat nail clippers work well; if you decide on a grinder, battery-driven grinders are the safest.
- **Quality dog shampoo:** canine shampoo must be used because a dog's skin chemistry is different from a human's; a small bottle of tearless canine shampoo can be useful for cleaning the head since most Chis object to washing their little faces.
- **Rubber bathmat:** place on the floor of the tub so your Chi doesn't slip; can be bought in the kitchenware or bathroom supplies of your local home goods store.
- **Small spray bottle:** for spraying coat conditioner.
- **Soft bristle brush:** made with soft natural bristles, this brush will not hurt your Chi's skin.
- **Styptic powder or pads:** to stop the bleeding if you accidentally cut your dog's nails too short.

A metal comb will help you get rid of mats.

- **Toothbrush and doggie toothpaste:** dog toothpaste is flavored for your dog's taste; human toothpaste has an ingredient that should not be swallowed by dogs. Dog toothbrushes come in small sizes to fit into a Chi's tiny mouth.
- **Washcloth or small sponge:** to apply shampoo to the face.

If you have a long-coated Chihuahua, you'll need a few extra things, including:

- **Fine-tooth comb/flea-type comb:** fine metal teeth are for finishing the coat and to check for overlooked mats.
- **Small pin brush:** a brush with metal teeth supported by a soft backing so it's flexible and won't tear the coat.
- **Thinning shears:** used around the ruff and the pants, etc.

Some optional supplies include:

- **Caddy or tote to keep supplies together:** keeps supplies in one convenient place.
- **Eye drops:** dropped in the eyes to keep them lubricated and free of shampoo.
- **Grooming loop:** helps to control the Chi and keep him from jumping off the table and injuring himself.
- **Grooming post:** to attach a grooming loop.
- **Grooming table or other table:** you can attach a groomer's post and loop to steady and control the dog.
- **Handheld pet hair dryer:** to dry your dog after bathing so he won't get a chill;

human dryers can become too hot and burn the skin.

- **Rubber brush:** soft, rubbery brush that's good for running over the smooth coat; it pulls out dead hair and dandruff and thoroughly invigorates the skin. Dogs love the feeling!

COAT AND SKIN CARE

Chihuahuas, those with both smooth and long coats, will only shed a little. However, his coat collects pollen and dust all year long, because he's so low to the ground. Weed bits and little dust-bunnies can get caught in a long-coated Chihuahua's fur. Even if your Chihuahua spends the majority of his time indoors, he'll be affected by anything on the floor, carpet, or any surface he comes in contact with. Brushing and bathing will help keep his coat tamed and free of dirt, and frequent brushing also means less hair on your furniture and clothes. And if you sleep with your Chi (and I know many of you do), there will be less dog hair in the bed.

BRUSHING

Your dog's hair follicles have a gland that produces oil. Brushing distributes the oil, which keeps the hair from drying out. Brushing also loosens the dirt that can become trapped close to the skin, under the hair. Trapped dirt can cause skin irritation. Brushing also removes any debris caught in the coat.

You should brush your long-coated Chi *at least* once a week to keep him mat- and dander-free. And even though your smooth-coated Chi doesn't look like he may need it, you should still brush him weekly in order to distribute oil and remove dirt.

How to Brush Your Chihuahua

- For a long-coated Chihuahua, mix a little doggie conditioner with water in a spray bottle and mist the coat before brushing to stop static and hair breakage. Many pet owners aren't concerned about a little hair breakage, but if you are going to do conformation showing, you will want a nice coat. You do not want a choppy looking coat in the ring.
- Then use a pin brush and brush out from the skin following the direction of the hair growth.
- For a smooth coat you can skip the first step; use a small, soft-bristle brush and work the brush from the skin out to the end of the hair shaft following the hair growth.
- Make sure the furnishings and the pants or britches on the long coat are

combed through, and all dirt and fecal matter are combed out.

- Check the hair under the ears, between the legs, and around the genital area—these areas are prone to matting. Start with a pin brush and finish with the comb to make sure you can run the comb's teeth all the way through the hair.
- Comb through the coat after brushing (getting down to the skin) to make sure all the tangles are removed
- Try not to pull too much on the skin. The Chi has sensitive skin, and it can be damaged easily. Being too rough with your Chihuahua will make him less than willing for the next grooming session.

Use a pin brush to brush a longer-coated Chi.

Dealing With Mats

The biggest grooming issue for longer-haired Chis is matting. Many hairs knotted together make up a mat. Luckily, those tangles can be taken care of with a visit to the kitchen. If you are having a hard time loosening a mat, apply a little bit of cornstarch on your comb, or apply cornstarch directly to the dry mat. This loosens the fur and makes the comb glide through the hair easily. Rub the cornstarch into the mat, and with your comb work the knot gently out. Hold on to the dog's skin (holding on to the handful of skin under the mat keeps you from pulling on the skin, which can be extremely painful) and comb from the hair tips. After you've loosened up the end of the snarl, work your way toward the skin until the mat is out. Like most things you do with your Chihuahua, this should be a gradual process, so be patient and keep it safe and pain-free. You can buy mat splitters at your pet retailer if all else fails.

The best way to avoid mats in the first place is to brush and comb your Chi regularly! This will keep you from having to cut out mats with scissors, which is a dangerous maneuver. Your dog's skin may be accidentally cut while trying to cut the snarl out. If you really have no other course, then slip a metal comb under the mat—between the skin and scissors. This keeps you from unintentionally cutting the skin. Or, an even better way to handle this is to take your Chi to a professional groomer before you resort to cutting out mats.

BATHING

You'll only need to bathe your Chihuahua about once a month—or less. If you need to do so more often (say he gets into something smelly or stinky), once a week is acceptable as long as you use a mild natural shampoo or a moisturizing one. In between baths, use pet wipes or dry shampoo to keep your Chi clean.

Chis are small enough to wash in most sinks, and you may find a sink easier on your back and knees. If you have trouble handling your dog in a sink, use the tub—it's less dangerous if he jumps out. Before you start, put a bathmat down in your sink or tub to make it less slippery, so that your Chihuahua feels more secure. You know how it feels to slip in the shower and grab at anything to keep from going down. If this happens to your Chi, he'll be grabbing at you with those sharp nails.

Keep one hand on your Chihuahua at all times when he's in the sink. They are fast, and many Chis don't like to get wet—they can jump out of a sink and land hard. A grooming loop placed over his head and one leg can be attached to your water spigot to help keep him in one place, but you still have to hold the dog. If he tries to jump out of the sink wearing the loop he could potentially hang himself.

How to Bathe Your Chihuahua

- Put your supplies next to the sink where you can reach everything.
- Brush your Chi before his bath to get out any tangles or mats.
- Put small cotton balls in your dog's ears to keep moisture out. You can tear the cotton balls into smaller puffs if they are too bulky to fit. Moisture in the ears makes fertile ground for bacteria, which can lead to ear infections.
- Check the temperature of the water against your hand. If the water is too hot, it can scald the skin and dry out the coat.
- Use a hose attachment to wet your dog, or use a scoop to pour water over the dog.
- Apply a line of shampoo down his back, add water, and lather well.
- Make sure to massage shampoo under his tail and belly, and don't forget to work soap into the pads of his foot; do his head last.
- Take a wet washcloth or sponge and add a dot of tearless shampoo to it. Work it around his face, taking care not to get soap into his nose.
- Hold your Chihuahua's head with his chin tilted up with one hand and use the

other to rinse off his face. This is where the puppy handling comes in handy. If you've trained your Chi to allow you to keep his head tipped up, this will keep the rinse water out of his nose. You don't want to let any water drip down his nose and into his lungs.

- Shield his eyes with your fingers when rinsing his face. Chis just don't like seeing that water rush toward their eyes. Try to keep water from going down his ears.
- Rinse under his tail, between his legs, and his feet. Rinse your Chi thoroughly, rinse, rinse, and rinse some more. Rinse until your head spins like the drain in the sink. If you don't get all the shampoo out of his hair, it will become irritating and start an itch-n-scratch cycle that you really don't want to begin.

With a few baths, you will have mastered washing your Chi; especially his head, which can be the most difficult part. Be patient—he'll want to get away fast after the first few baths, but if you are gentle and calm he'll get used to it.

Drying

Put your wet Chi on your designated grooming table. If you don't have a grooming table, dry him on the floor with a leash attached to a doorknob. (Never leave your dog on a table unattended, even to take a step away—he's faster than you are and can fall off or try to jump off.)

Dry your Chi with a fluffy towel to blot his coat, then use a handheld pet dryer. Don't be tempted to use a human blow dryer. It may seem convenient, but your Chi has thin, sensitive skin that can be irritated or burned by a human blow dryer. Pet blow dryers are the perfect temperature and air pressure to dry your Chihuahua quickly.

When drying a long-coat Chihuahua, don't put the dryer nozzle right up to his fur. Keep it about a foot (30 cm) or more away and blow the air in the direction his coat grows. This will help to minimize coat tangling. Brush your Chi again to smooth down his coat.

Dry your Chi with a fluffy towel.

Finishing Touches

For anyone showing their Chihuahua, there are a few more steps to take. Chihuahuas are supposed to be a natural breed, but that doesn't mean they should be scruffy. Owners usually trim their Chis before a show. The trick is to make them look natural; you really shouldn't be able to tell they've been groomed. They shouldn't be "sculpted," but they should have some basics done: a cleaned up muzzle, a trim around the base of the tail, neck enhanced, underbelly cleaned up, pants smoothed, and hair trimmed from the pads of the feet up to the hocks.

You may not want to go this far, or you may want a professional to help you get this cleaned-up look. A groomer can even show you how to trim a long-coated Chihuahua's "bump"—the wave of hairs that can curl up and stick up off the back. It just takes some thinning shears to thin the hair until the topline is smooth.

The ruff is another area that commonly needs trimming on the long-coated Chihuahua. The neck can often get lost in the ruff, making the dog look like he has no neck. Use thinning shears and do V-formations going down under the chin, taking a little bit of hair out to accentuate the neck. Chis are supposed to have a nice neck and an arch. If the ruff isn't done right, it can look like the head is sitting directly on the shoulders, like a body builder or a "no-neck" linebacker! Again, this is something a groomer can take care of, or show you how to do properly.

DENTAL CARE

Chis frequently have problems with tooth loss and gum disease so dental care is critical for this breed. With small dogs, their teeth tend to be squished into their smaller mouths, which creates dental problems. The first step to good dental care is getting your Chihuahua used to having his mouth handled. Start this process as soon as you bring your Chi home. Put your dog in your lap and rub his face, then lips, then slowly work into his mouth and massage his gums. Dogs enjoy the feel of gum massage, and when they relax, it will allow you to handle their mouths. Do this on a daily basis, and your dog will learn to accept it.

BRUSHING YOUR CHIHUAHUA'S TEETH

- Use a small dog toothbrush or a fingertip toothbrush, which can be less obtrusive and fit into a small dog's mouth more easily than a full-sized toothbrush.
- Make sure you use dog toothpaste; don't get out your human toothpaste. Dog toothpaste is flavored for dogs, which encourages him to accept it, and it is safe to swallow.
- You can brush his teeth with him on your lap, or have him stand on the grooming table.

Dog Tale

Scarlet was a tiny, fragile-looking Chi who had all the groomers at my dog grooming salon gushing over her when she was brought in to be groomed for the first time. After I brushed her, I walked her to the tub. That's when the bath battle began, and everyone in the shop realized that Scarlet was no pushover. She fought like a little banshee to keep from getting wet. It was as if she thought she would dissolve in water. She tried to claw her way up my legs, and once I finally got her in the tub she went for my arms and chest. She cried and then started screaming—literally. It's a good thing the windows were closed because we would not have been able to convince someone listening from outside that we weren't torturing her! Wet and miserable, she shook violently and made us all feel like brutes for subjecting her to the bath. I believe she must have taken acting lessons! Actually, she could give acting lessons because she was so convincing in her misery.

- Brush each tooth on all sides, making sure to get the teeth in the back of the mouth.
- Be gentle with brushing, but be thorough.

Brush once a week, or as often as your veterinarian recommends, based on your dog's individual dental needs. Brushing your Chi's teeth regularly will improve his breath and keep his teeth cleaner and healthy. While you are brushing, look at his teeth and gums. If the gums are red or swollen, this points to tartar and plaque buildup. In addition to your home preventative measures, your vet will check your Chi's teeth at his yearly wellness exam.

EAR CARE

Make ear inspections a part of your total grooming routine. It's something that takes a few minutes, but cleaning out dirty ears can prevent ear infections. If you think a problem is developing, go to the veterinarian. Left untreated, an ear infection can damage your dog's hearing.

CLEANING YOUR CHIHUAHUA'S EARS
- Clean out ears with a commercial liquid ear cleaner that can be obtained at your pet supply store or online. Be sure to follow the instructions on the bottle carefully.

- Use a cotton ball. Don't use ear swabs! Those ears are delicate and won't take a swab down the ear canal.
- Use a different cotton ball for each ear. That way, if one ear is infected, you won't transfer bacteria from one ear to the other.
- Do not ever shove the cotton ball deep into the canal; be gentle. Clean only where you can see.

A safe, alternate way to clean ears is to fill the ear with the cleaning solution then gently massage the base of the ear. Let the Chi shake his head to clear out the dirt.

EYE CARE

If your Chi is light-coated, you may find tear stains under his eyes and even down his cheeks. Caused by excess tearing, these stains can result in bacteria and red yeast growing on the moist area under the eyes.

Tear stains can make a gorgeous Chi face look forlorn and feel a bit gooey. There are some all-natural products on the market today that can be effective at battling tear stains. Premoistened eye pads are one option; you use them to wipe the stained area. To discourage eye stains, wipe under your Chi's eyes daily with premoistened wipes and keep the area dry.

To discourage eye stains, wipe under your Chi's eyes daily with premoistened wipes and keep the area dry.

NAIL CARE

Nails should be ground down or trimmed every two weeks or so. If you stick to a routine, the nails will never grow long enough to become uncomfortable to the dog. Long, grown-out nails can be torn or ripped out of the dog's foot. To avoid injuries, always keep the nails trimmed.

Small cat nail clippers are great for use on toy dogs; the larger ones can be unwieldy. If you use nail clippers, make sure the blades are sharp. Dull nail clippers will squeeze and tear the nails painfully.

One thing that new owners find scary about trimming their dog's nails is cutting the quick. The quick is the nerve that runs inside the nail. It will bleed and cause pain if it is cut. The quick can be easily seen in white nails, but not in black nails.

If you decide the risk of making your Chi bleed by using clippers is too much, try using a small battery-driven grinder. Grinders not only trim the nail, but smooth out the rough edges. To accustom your dog to the sound and vibration of a grinder run it over his body starting from his behind. Take care not to allow the spinning shaft to grab any hair because it will spin into the Chi's skin and cause injury.

TRIMMING YOUR CHIHUAHUA'S NAILS

- The most important tip is to remain calm and go slowly.
- Sit on a sofa or chair with the armrest next to you. This keeps the dog from sliding back to get away.
- Hold the dog firmly and close to your body. Put him in the cuddle position with your arm under the abdomen.
- Hold the leg you want to trim.
- When your Chi relaxes, run the nail clippers over his body then trim one nail, being careful not to cut the quick.
- Wait for your Chi to relax, then trim the next nail, and so on.
- If your Chi squirms, don't let him go! Just wait until he relaxes and calmly proceed with one nail only.

If you're having trouble with nail trimming, try the following:

- Hold your Chihuahua wrapped in a towel with one foot out; wait until he relaxes and proceed as above.
- Have someone else stand and hold the dog firmly in their arms, close to their body. Then reach under the body to do one nail at a time. The holder should be experienced with dogs because a panicked Chihuahua may try to bite.
- Take your Chi to a dog groomer who is trained to deal with dogs who don't want their nails trimmed.

FINDING A PROFESSIONAL GROOMER

Good groomers will have a good reputation, so check with your friends and ask your veterinarian for a referral. If you are new to town, check the Internet or the yellow pages of your local directory. Call the groomer and make an appointment to see the shop. Also, ask for references from the groomer (and check them!). Go tour the shop at the groomer's convenience. Keep in mind the groomer may be too busy at certain times of the day, and having strangers walking through the

BE AWARE!

The anal glands can become impacted in little dogs and need to be expressed. Leave anal gland expression to the professionals—this is a job for your veterinarian or groomer. You can rupture the anal glands if they are not expressed correctly, which can lead to extreme pain for your Chi and costly surgery. If you see your Chi constantly licking his bottom, or if he drags his rear-end on the carpet, it's time to visit your vet or groomer.

shop may upset the dogs, so be considerate of the business schedule.

Ask the groomer what types of shampoos she uses. Are the shampoos formulated for dogs? Does she have specialized shampoos for problem skin and coats? If you prefer a natural shampoo, does she supply it? Ask how long your dog will be expected to stay at his appointment. Some groomers have the luxury of working with one dog from the time he arrives, straight through to the end. This is time-consuming, so expect to pay more for your dog's grooming if this is the case. However, most groomers need to work like an assembly line, where one dog is washed and dried as the next is started. When you visit, see how the groomer handles the dogs. Is she gentle and caring, or too rushed and rough?

You can always ask the groomer if she is familiar with Chihuahuas, but a good groomer will know how to handle any breed and be familiar with most skin and coat conditions. The Chi doesn't generally have any breed-specific grooming needs other than what is common to many breeds, like allergies. A better idea would be to observe how the groomer interacts with small dogs—does she treat them with respect and care?

Signs of a good groomer include:

• A clean shop that smells fresh. Don't expect the shop to be hospital sterile, but it should have no odor of urine or poop.
• Professional cages and dryers.
• Someone who greets both you and your dog when you arrive. This is a sign of someone who doesn't just think of your dog as an object strictly to make money.

CHAPTER 6

HEALTH OF YOUR CHIHUAHUA

C hihuahuas generally are healthy dogs, and your Chihuahua will most likely live with you for quite some time. In fact, your children may grow up and move away while your Chihuahua remains in the home—devoted only to you! Chihuahuas usually live into their late teens, and there are reports of some Chis living to the age of twenty and beyond. With good care and preventative health measures, you can give your Chihuahua a chance of living long and well.

VETERINARY CARE

Finding the right veterinarian for your Chihuahua should be one of the first things you do when you decide to bring a new dog into your home. You should take your puppy to your vet within the first three days of bringing him home to make sure he's healthy. Many breeders want you to take your new puppy to the vet within 24 hours of getting him to validate the health guarantee. If you got your Chi from a conscientious breeder, you will have a genetic health guarantee and a general health guarantee, meaning the pup is free of diseases and the parents of the puppy have been tested for those genetic health problems that are common to Chihuahuas. While it's not a foolproof promise that the puppy won't develop a genetic ailment, it ups the odds that your Chi will stay free of them.

If you rescued your Chi, you may not have to visit the vet immediately. Some rescues have veterinarians perform health checks, spay/neuter, and vaccinations. A well-run rescue should supply you with the health documentation.

FINDING A VET

One of the most important issues with Chihuahuas is finding a vet who's knowledgeable about the breed. I've heard stories from Chi owners about vets telling them that their Chi is terribly unhealthy because of the dog's open fontanel (which naturally occurs in the breed). This means that the vet is not well informed and may

It's important to find a vet who's knowledgeable about your breed.

PUPPY POINTER

I was speaking to a breeder friend on the phone whose Chihuahua had given birth to puppies. I could hear the Chihuahua puppies playing in the background and they sounded like birds or mice to me. They are so tiny the barks sounded like "squeak, squeak." I could see how they might be mistaken for prey with that sound—they sounded like mice or birds! While those tiny squeaks are endearing, those puppies had to be kept in a very secure area—a loose dog, family cat, or other predator could do them serious harm, thinking they were prey.

even have a prejudice against the breed. You need to find a veterinarian who stays current and doesn't hold outdated ideas. To find the right vet for your Chi:

- If you got your puppy locally, use the same vet that your Chihuahua breeder uses. This will create continuity of care; plus, the vet will be familiar with your puppy's family's health concerns. (Most breeds and lines of dogs have genetic health issues in their family tree.)
- Call the secretary of the local breed club and find out which veterinarians the members use, or if they have recommendations of vets who have experience with toy dogs.
- Go to dog shows—these are good places to educate yourself. Find a breeder/owner who lives in your area and is showing her Chihuahua and ask for a recommendation. (Make sure to be respectful of her time—if she's getting ready for a class she may be rushed, so try and catch her at a more relaxed moment.)
- Get referrals from neighbors who are happy with their vet, or look for breed referral agencies.
- Go online to a search engine and type in "veterinarian" and your location. Many of the listings for your area will have reviews.

WHAT TO LOOK FOR

When you've narrowed down your search, it's time to make an appointment to visit the veterinarian's office. Consider the following:

- Is the location of the office convenient?
- What are the prices of services?
- Is the staff friendly and professional?
- Does the vet have experience with toy dogs in general and Chihuahuas in particular?

- Are anesthetics used for routine procedures, such as X-rays? (Because Chihuahuas are a toy dog, they should never be routinely anesthetized.)
- Does the office offer emergency services? If not, who will they refer you to in case of emergency? (You don't want to wait until the middle of the night on a holiday to search for one.)
- Does the vet work in conjunction with alternative therapy practitioners?

Find a vet who genuinely cares about dogs and with whom you have a good rapport. A comfortable relationship with your vet will help in times of crisis. You really don't want a vet who is in practice solely for the money; a vet who loves animals and loves helping animals is the right one to care for your Chihuahua.

ANNUAL VISIT

You'll be taking your puppy to see the veterinarian frequently in his first few months at home, since he'll need his series of vaccinations. After that, a yearly checkup will suffice. Yearly wellness check-ups are a great way for your vet to catch little problems before they become serious. Plus, they keep you up to date on your dog's changing needs as he ages. At the wellness check, your vet will examine your Chihuahua from nose to tail. If any health concerns are noticed the vet will address them and advise you if you need to take action.

Extra care needs to be taken with your Chi's teeth. They need to be checked often because Chihuahuas tend to have oral problems if not attended to. Sometime after your pup's first 6 months have your vet examine your dog's teeth to make sure the permanent teeth have come in correctly, and have her advise you on a dental plan for your dog.

VACCINATIONS

Your breeder should have taken care of your Chihuahua's initial puppy vaccinations, and will give you a written record that you can take to the veterinarian for the first visit. Your veterinarian will then be able to discuss with you the follow-up vaccines your pup will need. If you adopted your Chi, make sure to get the documentation of vaccinations and de-wormings from the rescue organization so you can bring them to your vet.

TYPES OF VACCINES

Vaccines are now generally categorized as *core* (recommended) and *noncore* (optional).

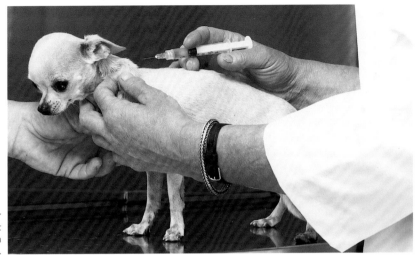

You should follow your vet's advice when it comes to vaccination protocols.

Core

Core vaccines are those that all dogs should receive in one form or other because they are essential protection from deadly diseases. Dogs don't actually need to be in direct contact with other canines to contract some of these diseases—some remain in the environment for years. Core vaccines include canine parvovirus, canine distemper, canine adenovirus-2, and rabies.

Noncore

Noncore vaccines are optional and include bordetella, distemper-measles, and leptospirosis. Bordetella is a vaccine against kennel cough and is usually recommended if your dog is in high-risk areas such as dog parks. Plus, most boarding facilities and doggy daycares require it. Leptospirosis is a virus that is not a big risk in every area of the country. The vaccine has been linked to adverse reactions. You need to talk to your veterinarian about the risk in your area and decide whether it is worth the risk to get the shot.

FREQUENCY

What vaccines your dog needs and how often to vaccinate are subjects of controversy. Over-vaccinations have been implicated in complications such as injury, toxicity, and sensitivity reactions. However, it is worth the small risk of adverse reactions to protect your pet from deadly diseases.

Years ago, your veterinarian would have recommended a series of puppy vaccinations followed by annual boosters of the core vaccinations. After further testing and research, it was discovered that many vaccinations were sufficient for 3 years or longer. At the same time, it became increasingly clear that vaccines have the potential to cause many side effects. Although rare, complications and vaccine reactions can be life-threatening.

The American Animal Hospital Association (AAHA) Canine Vaccine Task Force (formed by experts in immunology, internal medicine, infectious diseases, and medical and clinical practitioners) developed a document to guide veterinarians in making vaccination decisions for their animal patients. The guidelines are supported by scientific and clinical evidence, as well as professional and published documentation.

The general recommendation is to vaccinate puppies with core vaccines to be followed up with booster shots when the dog is a year old. After that, the usual recommendation is boosters every 3 years. Rabies vaccinations are boostered at a year and then you must follow your local laws.

You can also talk to your veterinarian about vaccine serology, where they will take a blood sample from your dog and perform antibody *titer tests*. These tests can be used to check if acceptable vaccine defense still exists in your dog. Such testing isn't perfect, but generally it will indicate if there is active and sufficient protection, and therefore no need for vaccine boosters.

Discuss with your vet the specific vaccinations that your Chihuahua will need in your region. Certain vaccinations may be unjustified based on risk and lifestyle factors. For instance, if your Chihuahua rarely leaves your home and/or is always carried, his lifestyle carries low risk of being exposed to diseases that other dogs might encounter while walking in public. Some of these diseases pose less of a risk than the vaccines do, and treating the dog if he becomes ill is less threatening to his health than the vaccine.

Have your Chihuahua's health records available to show to your vet and discuss what is recommended for your dog's particular lifestyle. You should follow your vet's advice when it comes to vaccination protocols.

SPAY/NEUTER

Spaying or neutering is beneficial to your Chihuahua's health—for both genders. It reduces the chances of female dogs getting breast cancer and males getting prostate cancer. Spaying or neutering will keep your female Chi from getting pregnant or your male from impregnating females. It will lessen a male's desire to go out and roam. Altered dogs have an easier time adjusting to housetraining— intact males will mark their territory, including inside your home.

Spaying or neutering is beneficial to your Chihuahua's health.

Don't believe the myth that spay/neutering will change a Chi's attitude—they'll still be little spitfires—but without the unwanted aggression that sometimes shows up in unneutered males.

The only reason not to spay/neuter is if you plan to show and breed your dog. However, keep in mind that showing is an expensive and time-consuming sport, and most Chihuahuas don't measure up to the breed standard. And think twice before you decide to breed your Chi. Because of their size, Chihuahuas often have a hard time with delivery of puppies, which can be dangerous to the mom. Genetic screening is also necessary before you breed to make sure of the dog's soundness. Breeders strive to contribute to the betterment of the breed, which is very costly. For these reasons, it's probably best to leave breeding to the experts.

CHIHUAHUA-SPECIFIC PROBLEMS

Chihuahuas are usually robust dogs, however they can have breed-specific health concerns as puppies and adults. Responsible breeders work hard to eliminate health issues, but no breed is totally without them. Listed here are several health problems (some serious, some not), that are seen in Chihuahuas.

COLLAPSING TRACHEA

Collapsing trachea is seen in many toys dogs. It is a genetic condition that affects

the soft cartilage and connective tissue in the windpipe. The rings of the windpipe fall inward, which narrows the opening and causes the dog to have hard time breathing. Think of the windpipe as a straw that delivers air to the chest; when the straw collapses, breathing gets difficult.

If a Chihuahua displays labored breathing, or acts faint or gasps for breath after excitement or exercise, he may have a collapsing trachea. After an attack, the dog may be exhausted and exhibit coughing.

Talk to your vet about the problem. In milder cases, management and certain medications can help. Collapsing trachea can be aggravated by collars that can put pressure on the neck of the Chihuahua. This is why many vets recommend a harness for walking your Chi. If you are a smoker, the second-hand smoke can also contribute to the problem—the smoke settles down by your Chihuahua and can make it hard for him to breathe.

HYDROCEPHALUS

Hydrocephalus is a neurologic disease that occurs from an excess accumulation of cerebrospinal fluid within the brain. The drainage system malfunctions and doesn't drain the cerebrospinal fluid from the brain into the circulatory system. It causes swelling in the brain and can result in brain damage and death. It occurs in puppies under 9 months of age or dogs over 6 years. The most common cause of hydrocephalus in young animals is congenital defect.

Toy breeds have the highest incidence of hydrocephalus. Chihuahuas have an average number of "hydro" pups, but some vets assume that, because of the molera, the Chihuahua is more prone to hydrocephalus. The current consensus, as supported by the Chihuahua Club of America (CCA), is that moleras do not increase the incidence of hydrocephalus. An experienced vet can help distinguish between a normal molera and hydrocephalus.

Breeders often keep Chihuahua puppies until they are older than the usual 8 weeks of age to ensure that they don't have hydrocephalus.

HYPOGLYCEMIA

Chihuahuas face a heightened risk of hypoglycemia, or low blood sugar. Toy dog puppies can be especially susceptible to hypoglycemia because of their size—they can't store or activate very much glucose. This is one reason why many Chihuahua breeders keep their puppies until they are older; many larger breed puppies are allowed to go to their new home at 8 weeks of age. Most Chis outgrow the problem, but sometimes in the tiniest of the tiny it can remain a threat.

Symptoms of hypoglycemia include a lurching gait, glassy eyes, seizures, and then unconsciousness. If the dog isn't helped immediately he may die.

Treatment includes putting something sugary in his mouth or dabbing honey on his gums and heading to the vet clinic. Hypoglycemia can happen with alarming swiftness, so be sure to have a tube of a high-sugar supplement in your first aid kit. It can save your Chi's life. Think about conditioning your Chi to take sugary water from an eyedropper in case he ever becomes hypoglycemic. Do this before you find yourself in a critical situation.

If your Chihuahua is predisposed to hypoglycemia, you must prevent further problems by managing his food intake. Change his feeding schedule to small amounts fed several times throughout the day. Limit the sugar intake in his food and treats so he's not on a roller-coaster of blood sugar highs and lows; you need to keep his blood sugar stable. There are several products on the market to feed to your Chihuahua that have the right balance of ingredients, including a high-energy supplement that can be fed to your Chi to keep up his blood sugar levels if he is off his food or is prone to hypoglycemia. A formula is available for both puppies and dogs. Other products you can use in a pinch are normal sources of sugar—corn or maple syrup and honey. These simple sugars should not be fed every day as they can cause dogs to be more susceptible to hypoglycemia.

Several factors can precipitate the onset of hypoglycemia, including stress; low body temperature; poor nutrition; sudden change in feed, water, and schedule patterns; infections; and premature birth. Some puppies, bred exclusively for tiny size ("teacup Chihuahuas"), are even more predisposed to transient juvenile hypoglycemia since insufficient muscle mass may make

Chihuahuas are usually healthy dogs, but there are a few breed-specific health concerns.

it difficult for the body to store glucose and keep its blood sugar properly regulated.

LUXATING PATELLA

Luxating patella, sometimes called a *slipped stifle* or *loose kneecap*, is a dislocation of the flat bone at the front of the knee. Luxating patellas are seen in the rear legs as the kneecap slips out of its groove in the bone. The problem is more common in toy dogs and can be the result of a congenital malformation or injury.

Luxating patellas can usually be detected when a puppy is taken to his first veterinarian check; the vet will feel the rear kneecaps to see if they are stable or loose. Symptoms include intermittent hopping or limping, due to the kneecap sliding out of place. Mild cases may not cause pain, but the problem may worsen with age and wear and tear. The condition can be corrected by surgery in cases in which the dog has pain and frequent slipping of the knee. Luxating patella can be aggravated by excess weight. All the more reason to keep your Chihuahua at his recommended weight.

MOLERA

Chihuahuas can be born with an opening—a soft spot—at the top of the skull. Known as the *molera* or *open fontanel*, it makes the skull more flexible, which allows the Chi's oversized head to emerge as he is born. The soft spot can close as the dog matures, but in some cases, moleras only partially close or don't close at all. History indicates that the molera was required in Chihuahuas in the past, but it's no longer necessary to prove the dog is a purebred.

Extra care must be taken with any Chi who retains the molera. Treat a molera Chihuahua as you would an infant with a correspondingly normal opening in the skull (in humans, this is called the *fontanel*). Handle them gently and guard them from roughness. Do not allow small children to handle them, and discourage any form of rough play.

Aside from these extra precautions, moleras very rarely cause problems in dogs. Some veterinarians may diagnose the soft spot incorrectly as hydrocephalus (water on the brain), but the presence of a molera doesn't mean the Chihuahua is ill.

OBESITY

Some Chihuahuas have a propensity to become overweight. Obesity is a major cause of heart disease and can affect your Chihuahua's length and quality of life. To maintain proper weight, make sure he gets regular exercise, including daily walks. Keep him on a healthy, nutritious diet and avoid high-fat, high-calorie treats. If your Chi is overweight, even if you are restricting calories and exercising, then a visit to the vet is called for.

PERIODONTAL DISEASE

Chihuahuas are prone to periodontal problems, so dental care is necessary to prevent diseases and bad breath. Chihuahuas are prone to loss of teeth and gum diseases, which could develop into serious conditions like bacterial infections of the heart, kidneys, or liver.

Daily teeth brushing is recommended to help remove plaque and slow tartar buildup. Give your Chihuahua dental chews to help keep down the odor and massage his gums.

Talk to your veterinarian about teeth cleaning and how often your Chi should be checked. If you decide not to brush your Chihuahua's teeth, having the Chi's teeth professionally cleaned is not an option—it's a must.

REVERSE SNEEZING

Chihuahuas can develop reverse sneezing, a problem that is common among

If your Chi is overweight even if you are restricting calories and exercising, then a visit to the vet is called for.

A friend recalls a frightening moment with her first Chihuahua, Jules. "The first few months Jules lived with us, I started hearing this honking noise coming from him. It really startled me the first couple of times. I rushed him to the vet who told me that no, Jules wasn't part goose—he's definitely a purebred Chihuahua. He explained that some toy dogs have a problem called reverse sneezing and that Jules was healthy—I'd just have to get used to the honking. I didn't think it was so amusing at the time."

many small breeds. It has been described as gasping for air, wheezing, or honking sounds. Reverse sneezing can be caused by allergies, cold air, dust and pollen, or soft palate problems.

Generally, reverse sneezing is not a serious health issue. Watching it happen to your Chi, though, can be alarming because it looks and sounds so severe. The dog is not actually suffocating or choking. Air is being pulled in quickly through the nose and generating noisy results. Some owners have success stopping the episode by making the dog swallow by pulling gently on the tongue or massaging the throat. It generally lasts only for a few minutes and has no ill effects. Afterward the dog acts normally.

In dogs in whom this phenomena is frequent (daily or several times a day) and abnormal signs exist such as bloody nose, nasal discharge, difficulty breathing, lethargy, or decreased appetite, a trip to vet is advised to test for more serious causes, such as nasal mites and nasal cancer.

TOXIN SENSITIVITY

Chihuahuas live very close to the ground, and can easily pick up toxins from floors, carpets, and pesticides on lawns, which can be absorbed through the pads of the feet. Because they are always low to the ground and small, their exposure to toxins can be quite dangerous. To be prudent always use pet-safe products to clean your floors and carpets. If you suspect a grassy area has been treated with pesticides, don't allow your Chi to walk there.

If your Chi has been exposed to anything harmful, call the ASPCA Animal Poison Control Center (888-426-4435). They should be able to help in case of emergency.

GENERAL PROBLEMS

There are a few other illnesses and problems common to all dogs, including Chihuahuas.

EYE INJURIES

Chihuahuas are not more prone to vision problems than most dogs, but because they are so close to the ground and because their eyes are quite large, they are more susceptible to eye injuries that larger dogs usually avoid. Some owners get down at the Chihuahua's level and look around for possible hazards that need to be eliminated in the house.

KENNEL COUGH

Kennel cough is an illness that's spread from an infected dog to other dogs, especially in environments where dogs socialize, such as dog parks and dog shows. The most common kind of kennel cough is called *Bordetella bronchiseptica*, which is a strain of kennel cough caused by bacteria. However, there is more than one kind of strain of kennel cough, including canine adenovirus, which is caused by a virus. Both can be airborne, and to be infected the dog must inhale it. It can be spread in doggy daycares or kennels, obedience classes, grooming salons, or even local dog parks. It is highly contagious, but not usually serious. An infected dog dry hacks and often sounds like he has something stuck in his throat.

Bordetella intranasal sprays are available, but need to be repeated twice a year because they're only effective for about 6 months. Bordetella vaccinations last longer, but still need to be given yearly. Some people use nasal sprays instead of vaccines because there is no pain involved, which can be important if you have a dog who is highly sensitive or fears the vet visit. The nasal spray is a live attenuated dose, which some studies say results in much quicker immunities. Some studies have called into question the effectiveness of the nasal spray. This is one of the many reasons why you need a good working relationship with your veterinarian, who should be well-informed to help you decide. Most grooming salons, kennels, or doggy daycares require dogs to have this vaccination to be allowed though the doors.

Coughing can be caused by problems other than kennel cough. It depends on each dog's specific situation. Symptoms like runny nose and coughing can be related to nasal irritation from inhaled irritants. Coughing can also be a symptom of more serious diseases like heartworms, heart conditions, tuberculosis, or distemper. For this reason, when coughing occurs, it's best to discuss the problem with your vet.

PARASITES

Parasites are a constant danger to your dog. External parasites can spread disease and leave your dog in a weakened state and more vulnerable to other illnesses.

Fleas

Fleas are the most common pest affecting dogs. Fleas live on dogs and feed on their blood. Some dogs have an allergic reaction to flea bites, which leaves the dog scratching himself raw. If your Chihuahua is miserable and continually scratching, check his skin for fleas. Look for a quick-moving dark insect (they can be hard to follow because they move so quickly!). If you wet the dog's coat in the bathtub, you can see little black specks jumping out of the coat. Often, you can see the signs they leave behind more easily than the fleas themselves—areas of dark flea feces on the dog's skin composed of digested blood.

After you identify fleas as the problem, eliminating them from your dog is relatively easy by giving him a bath with special flea shampoo. Then you must treat the environment as well, or your Chi-Chi will be re-infested, and if left long enough, you may be bitten by fleas. There are many products on the market to help you rid your dog and your home of fleas. There are flea soaps, sprays, and collars, and preventative spot-on liquids applied between the shoulder blades. Wash or replace all the dog's bedding, and clean carpets, furniture, and the spaces underneath all your furniture.

Start with a complete vacuuming and mopping of floors. Discard the used vacuum bag. Then treat the entire area with flea killer. Different products kill different stages of flea development. Follow the manufacturer's directions to know when a follow-up treatment is necessary. A yard insecticide may be recommended for outside.

Ticks

Ticks are a problem in temperate and humid climates and anywhere wildlife lives. Even if you live in a cool area, your dog can get ticks from a walk in the woods. Dog ticks can't fly or jump like fleas do, but they can crawl long distances to reach a dog. Ticks suck a dog's blood and can spread diseases like Lyme disease and Rocky Mountain Spotted tick fever. If a dog has a heavy infestation of ticks, he can become weakened and debilitated. Inspect your dog's skin thoroughly after he's been in grassy or wooded areas. Many powders, shampoos, and sprays are effective, but the best prevention is frequent checks and the removal of ticks.

Check your dog for fleas and ticks after he's been outside.

Worms

Heartworms, hookworms, roundworms, tapeworms, and whipworms are parasites that can infect dogs.

• **Heartworms** are parasites that can infect your dog's heart and can kill your dog. Heartworms are easy to prevent in dogs; however, they are problematic and expensive to cure. Heartworms are transmitted from infected dogs courtesy of mosquito bites. The mosquito drinks the blood of the infected dog, the larva incubate and develop in the mosquito, and then are passed on to other dogs when they are bitten. Once in the dog's bloodstream, they migrate to the heart, surrounding blood vessels and lungs. The symptoms include loss of appetite and energy, coughing, and anemia. Currently, vets recommend preventative care by starting your puppy on medication before he is exposed to the parasite. Blood tests can be used for the older dog or rescue who has not previously been on the preventative medication. Your vet will do a blood test to check for heartworms, and she can offer medications to eliminate and prevent these worms from infecting your dog.

• **Hookworms** are parasites that live in the digestive system of dogs. The worm uses its teeth to hook to the lining of the small intestines and feed on the dog's blood. Hookworms can cause inflammation of the intestines and anemia. The eggs of the hookworm are expelled in the dog's feces. The larvae hatch from the eggs, and from there they permeate the soil and contaminate the environment. They can infect your dog (and people) through contact with and penetration of the skin, including through the paws, as well as getting ingested when the dog licks his paws. Puppies get hookworms from an infected mother's milk. Heavy infections can be fatal in puppies. Dogs with hookworms often have a poor appetite, weakness, weight loss, anemia, and pale membranes. If the parasite gets into the lungs, it will cause coughing. Other symptoms are diarrhea and a tarry stool or constipation. Hookworms cannot be seen with the eye; your vet can see them under the microscope. Luckily, medication from your vet will rid your dog of these parasites. Chihuahua owners need to be conscientious in cleaning up dog feces and keeping dog areas clean and disinfected. Although hookworm cases are not common in humans, the parasites can penetrate human skin, so wash your hands.

- **Roundworms** are parasites that live in the digestive system of dogs and are shed constantly in the feces—they are the most common internal parasites. Roundworms are also infective to humans. They can be obtained in several ways, which makes them simple to spread and difficult to control. A mother dog can pass them to her puppies in utero, or after the puppy is born he can eat worm larva from the environment. If dogs eat mice or other infected small animals, they can contract roundworms. Frequently, you cannot tell if your dog is infected but some signs are potbelly, dull hair, coughing, and weight loss. Sometimes, you will see the worms in your dog's feces. They are brownish or white spaghetti-like worms that are several inches (cm) long. Talk to your vet about a good program for eliminating these parasites. Always keep your yard free of dog feces to help control worm infestations.

- **Tapeworms** are long, flat worms that attach to the dog's intestines. A tapeworm's body is segmented. These segments can usually be seen on the dog's anal opening, attached to his hair, or in his feces. They look like grains of rice. Dogs most often get tapeworms from fleas, so put your dog on a flea-preventative plan (as discussed with your vet). Dogs who eat wildlife, including mice, are often infested. Infected dogs can transmit tapeworms to people, so be hygienic. Dog's don't usually show obvious signs, such

You can have your Chi checked for worms during regular visits to the veternarian.

as illness or weight loss, when they have tapeworms. Your vet can test for tapeworms and offer treatment options.

- **Whipworms** are long thin worms (shaped like a whip) that live in the dog's colon and cause intestinal bleeding. Whipworms can be prevented by removing dog feces from the affected area. Whipworms are more difficult to diagnose than other parasites, so it is imperative to go to the vet at least annually for a fecal exam. Many dogs show no obvious symptoms. Heartworm medications that contain milbemycin oxime can be used prophylactically.

You can have your Chihuahua checked for worms during regular trips to the veterinarian. An annual (or more frequent if needed) fecal exam is recommend. One of the best preventatives is constant vigilance in sanitation of the dog's environment. Your vet can offer safe and effective dewormers to eradicate the common worms.

FIRST AID

As you live with your Chihuahua, you will observe his everyday habits and behavior and learn what is normal for him. This helps you to spot any sign of trouble and ward it off before it's an emergency.

TREATING MINOR PROBLEMS

Some minor injuries and illnesses can be treated at home, like stomach upset or a small cut. Sometimes dogs will have a little stomach upset when they overindulge or have eaten something that disagrees with them. Chis are so close to the ground that it's easy for them to vacuum up little things left on the floor as they roam around your house. A gastric upset can be brought on by nervousness or changing the dog's food. Withholding food for a meal and then feeding a bland diet of rice and cooked lean ground beef or chicken before allowing a normal meal will help in many cases. Vomiting or diarrhea that continues for more than 48 hours or that is extreme warrants a call to your veterinarian.

For a cut that's small and not deep, clean the wound with warm water and apply an antibiotic cream. For cuts that are deep, bleeding excessively, and/or are caused by foreign objects take your Chihuahua to the veterinarian quickly.

FIRST-AID KIT

A Chihuahua owner can treat minor injuries if you keep a first-aid kit filled with some remedies and tools. To be ready for any emergency that can happen, have a first-aid kit stocked and ready.

- **Baby/children's aspirin.** To treat a fever or pain until you can get the dog to a vet. Not to be used for a prolonged period. Do not use a human dosage—the general recommendation is one half a baby aspirin for a 5-pound (2 kg) Chihuahua. (Don't use Tylenol, as it is toxic to dogs.)

- **Children's liquid diphenhydramine.** To reduce symptoms of allergies. Also used to reduce mild reactions to insect bites or stings and some medications. If your Chi is having a more serious reaction, the diphenhydramine may buy you time to get your dog to the vet for treatment. Do not use the medication in human dosages. Ask your vet for the dosing guidelines for your Chihuahua.

A Chihuahua owner can treat minor injuries if you keep a first-aid kit handy.

- **Electrolyte solution.** To replace essential minerals and electrolytes lost due to diarrhea and vomiting; prevents dehydration. Available at the grocery store or drugstore.
- **Eye wash or saline solution.** For minor eye problems, to flush out foreign objects.
- **Gauze.** To wrap injuries.
- **High-calorie pet supplement, light corn syrup, or honey.** A source of sugar in case of hypoglycemia.
- **Muzzle.** To stop a dog from biting. A hurt or stressed dog may bite from panic if injured. If you don't have a muzzle, make an emergency muzzle from ribbon or a nylon stocking. Tie it around the Chi's muzzle, and then loop it over the top of the head. Never tie too tightly—you want your Chi to be able to breathe.
- **Oral syringe.** To give your Chi medications.
- **Paperwork.** Your regular vet's phone number and an emergency clinic's phone number. Include your dog's current medications and a health record. Also include the ASPCA's poison control phone number (888-426-4435).
- **Rescue Remedy.** A natural, flower-based remedy to help calm your Chihuahua if he is frightened or stressed. Use as directed.
- **Self-adhering athletic bandage.** To wrap injuries.

- **Sterile, non-adherent pads.** Used on injuries under wrap.
- **Styptic powder or pen.** To stop nail bleeding. You can use flour or corn starch for a natural remedy if you don't have another blood coagulation product.
- **Thermometer.** To take your Chi's temperature. A digital thermometer is recommended. (Normal temperature for dogs is between 101 and 102°F [38 and 39°C].)
- **Triple antibiotic ointment.** To treat minor cuts or scrapes. You should always take your dog to the veterinarian for serious cuts or bite wounds.
- **Tweezers.** To remove small stickers and ticks.

ALTERNATIVE MEDICINE

Alternative or complementary medicine uses a group of ancient methods to treat physical illnesses. Once considered unconventional, alternative medicine is now accepted in most of the veterinary community as a complement to conventional Western medicine. Alternative therapies include chiropractic care, homeopathic care, herbs, acupuncture, and massage. Many vets use these modalities in conjunction with traditional medicine. These practices can help relieve your Chi of pain, make him more comfortable, and help him recover from various conditions.

Alternative medicine can be used as a complement to conventional medicine..

One of the most common alternative practices, acupuncture, involves inserting fine needles into a specific area of a dog's body. It is often used to help manage chronic illnesses and control pain, including arthritis. It has even been used to strengthen a dog's immune function. This ancient Chinese practice may seem scary to some, but most dogs seem to find the whole thing painless.

If you are interested in alternative practices, make sure the practitioner you choose is certified or licensed by the governing body in the alternative therapy the practitioner wants to administer.

Ask your regular vet for referrals, and ask other dog owners who have been satisfied using an alternative therapist.

You can check with these organizations for more on alternative therapy:
- American Academy of Veterinary Acupuncture (AAVA): www.aava.org
- American Holistic Veterinary Medical Association (AHVMA): www.ahvma.org
- American Veterinary Chiropractic Association (AVCA): www.animalchiropractic.org
- Academy of Veterinary Homeopathy (AVH): www.theavh.org

SENIOR CHIHUAHUAS

There is no hard and fast rule about when your Chihuahua is considered "old"; there is no single age when Chihuahuas are considered senior. It can vary with the condition of your Chihuahua and the life he's lived. Generally, Chihuahuas can be considered seniors when they reach about 8 to 10 years of age. Health care, nutrition, exercise, and genetics can affect the lifespan of individuals. With good care, however, many Chis live into their teens.

SIGNS OF AGING

Old age is usually a gradual process of slowing down, both physically and mentally. Generally, most people notice their dog slowing in his usual activity. Sometimes a housetrained Chi will start having potty accidents or seem a little confused. Early signs your Chihuahua may be starting to feel his years can be as subtle as not eating as much, barking more often, or sleeping more than he used to. Other signs include loss of hearing or sight, graying of his coat, or disinterest in playing.

Sometimes a grouchiness that the dog didn't have before may indicate arthritis. If you start noticing changes in your Chihuahua's

Generally, Chihuahuas can be considered seniors when they reach about 8 to 10 years of age.

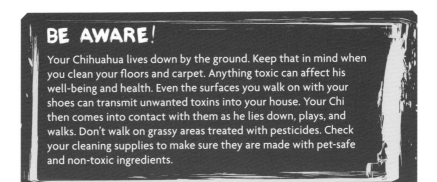

BE AWARE!

Your Chihuahua lives down by the ground. Keep that in mind when you clean your floors and carpet. Anything toxic can affect his well-being and health. Even the surfaces you walk on with your shoes can transmit unwanted toxins into your house. Your Chi then comes into contact with them as he lies down, plays, and walks. Don't walk on grassy areas treated with pesticides. Check your cleaning supplies to make sure they are made with pet-safe and non-toxic ingredients.

behavior, take him to the vet because many serious problems related to old age can be managed with proper care.

The immune system in senior dogs is not in its prime, and tumors can appear on a dog's body. While they look frightening, they are often benign. They are often fatty tumors that don't harm the dog (unless they are on a sensitive area or become infected). Have any bumps you notice on your senior Chi's body checked by his vet.

SENIOR WELLNESS EXAM

Senior Chihuahuas need some extra TLC to live out their golden years without pain. Dogs aren't able to let us know when they don't feel well, so it's essential to keep up with your dog's yearly wellness visits to the vet, and many vets recommend a twice-yearly exam. This way, your vet can detect problems early and recommend options for relieving pain and preventing illness. Ask your vet about any preventative programs she offers for senior dogs.

Your veterinarian will probably want to do some health screening. Luckily, senior dogs can be health tested in less invasive ways than previously used. Newer procedures and diagnostic tests are often shorter in duration and may be performed with only local anesthesia.

Ask your vet about possible changes to your senior's diet. The health of your older Chihuahua is very dependent on the food that he digests. To eat properly, the strength and structure of the teeth must be good. Hopefully, you've provided your Chi with good dental care and prevented tooth decay. Some older dogs won't be as eager to chew if their teeth are tender.

Older dogs have a greater need for consistency in their lives because of failing eyesight and hearing. They may be easily confused by changes. Have compassion for your Chihuahua as he ages and take better care of him than ever!

TRAINING YOUR
CHIHUAHUA

Many people who consider themselves dog lovers look down on toy dogs. How many times have you heard "I don't care for little dogs, I love *big* dogs"? There's a perception that little dogs are less of a "dog" because of their size. But anyone who believes Chis are somehow "less dog" must have never known one, because Chis make a big impact on their world. Let's just say this intelligent, take-charge breed can be more dog than most people can handle! That's why, just like their larger counterparts, Chihuahuas need to be trained in order to display to the world their best character.

WHY TRAIN YOUR CHIHUAHUA?

It's easy to think of your Chihuahua as a just a lapdog who doesn't need training. However, if you want to welcome friends and family into your home with any degree of comfort, you must train your Chihuahua. If you want a pleasant companion who is welcome anywhere you are, train your Chihuahua. And if you want to keep your little ball of energy safe, train your Chihuahua. After all, it only takes seconds for a dog to zip past you at the front door and run into traffic. You want a dog who'll listen to you when you say, "Come!" as he dashes out of that door.

Some Chihuahua owners never even get past potty training (that is, if they even get that far). Chis have a stubborn streak, and it's easy to give up before the dog is trained. Chis who have more willfulness or a terrier-like "mind of their own" can be difficult to train. However, Chis do want to please you, and if you persevere with training, you will end up with a well-mannered companion. Your Chi will be a joy to be around and a good representative of the breed. Plus, you can be proud of yourself for successfully training your Chi.

POSITIVE TRAINING

How you approach training can either facilitate success or create training headaches. The newer methods use positive training, as opposed to old-style punishment training. In the past, many trainers taught with force—jerking the dog around with choke chains and pushing him into the desired positions while shouting out commands. When the dog (not necessarily understanding what was wanted) failed, physical roughness was employed.

Positive training takes a different and more effective approach. A reward is used to lure a dog into performing the desired command. When the dog complies, the reward is given. Rewards can be whatever motivates the dog—praise, treats, play, or anything the dog values and sees as incentive to do the right thing.

Positive training is, as it name states, positively based. Rather than punishing the dog (causing physical pain or discomfort) when he does something you don't want him to, you ignore misbehavior (when you can) and reward or reinforce him when he does the correct thing. Positive training does not include force or loud, angry yelling.

Punishment-based training takes the fun out of training for you and your Chi and is more likely to be met with resistance from him. Positive training gives your Chihuahua the opportunity of cooperating with you—without force. The use of positive training methods will take your Chihuahua further in a shorter amount of time than any of the dated, harsh methods.

Punitive training techniques are not optimal for training any breed—and especially not for Chihuahuas, who are sensitive and can sustain injuries easily with severe methods. Harsh methods can actually work against training a Chihuahua because they can cause a failure to bond with your dog, and *bonding is the first step to successful training*. Punishment-based training creates either a timid, shy Chihuahua or a mean one—turning your dog into the stereotypical spiteful little toy. Worse, punishment-based training can make your Chi afraid of you.

TRAINING MISCONCEPTIONS

First of all, positive training does *not* mean that your Chi has no standards of behavior. It's not about letting your Chi do whatever he wants. Rather, positive

Using rewards (such as treats) makes training easy and enjoyable for both of you.

training sets up communication that leads to a rapport with your dog. It gives you the foundation to teach him proper behavior. Using positive methods will provide solid training, which makes you a good parent.

Another misconception is the belief that your dog will like you less if you teach him the rules. Every dog needs a frame of reference for proper behavior. This is the only way he'll understand how to fit happily into your life. You may end up surprised how much your Chi loves to learn, especially when you approach training in the correct way. He'll love you for the leadership and guidance training provides. Plus, knowing that you are in control gives your dog a feeling of security, which can stop him from becoming hypervigilant and nervous.

Take your puppy out and introduce him to new things in a safe and fun way.

Be patient, but consistent. Be gentle, but firm when needed. Don't baby or coddle your Chi when you are training him; expect your Chihuahua to be trained just like any canine. There is always time for cuddling after the lesson—it's a great reward for a job well done.

SOCIALIZATION

Socialization is introducing your Chihuahua to other dogs, people, and different situations so he is relaxed and able to mentally cope with anything new that comes his way. Socialization is a must on the "to-do" list for a well-balanced and socially secure Chihuahua.

A good breeder starts the socialization process while a puppy is still with his littermates. By handling the puppies and exposing them (in a limited way) to other people, the breeder lays a solid foundation for you to follow. Once your puppy comes home, continue to expand on your puppy's socialization. Now it's up to you to expose your Chi to different environments, people, and other dogs.

You most likely got your puppy between 8 and 12 weeks of age. The critical socialization period lasts until about 14 weeks of age. That leaves you with 2 to 6 weeks of time to start your Chi on the path to a stable temperament. If you wait until after he is over 14 weeks of age, you risk missing the best window of opportunity to socialize. While you can socialize a dog after this time (or even an older adopted dog), the process will be significantly more work and some shy dogs may never become totally comfortable.

The problem with the critical time frame is that your puppy will not have had his complete set of vaccinations, which poses some risks. If you decide to socialize your pup before his vaccinations are complete, only visit places where you know the dogs are safe and up-to-date on their vaccinations.

HOW TO SOCIALIZE

Start getting your Chi used to his collar and leash right away. Then take him out for a short walk down your block—stopping to talk to neighbors and letting your pup hear the noises and see the action of everyday life. If your pup becomes spooked at any point, don't move on; instead, show him with your unconcerned behavior that you are not worried and wait until he is relaxed, then reward him for his brave behavior. If you comfort your Chi while he's afraid, he will think you are approving of his fear.

Have your friends come over to meet and greet your puppy. If they have friendly, calm dogs of their own, encourage them to bring them. Talk to your neighbors who own small dogs and see if they would like to meet for a doggy play date or organize short neighborhood walks. Make sure you allow your puppy enough time with the strangers he meets to relax around them. If you introduce them and then quickly leave, your Chi may not have had enough time to adjust and he may become fearful. This will make it difficult the next time he faces a similar situation.

You, of course, need to keep your Chi safe during the socialization process. The key is to make new experiences fun and rewarding. Be aware, but not anxious. Your pup will look to you and pick up your feelings, so having a positive attitude toward other people and dogs is important. Dogs are talented at picking up their owner's emotions, so stay calm but be vigilant.

Socialization is like any other part of the training process: Work at your dog's level, bring him along slowly at his comfortable learning pace, and gradually he will be willing to meet anyone and go anywhere with you unconditionally. Your dog will trust both you and the world around you.

A puppy class can be helpful for socialization.

PUPPY CLASS

A puppy class can be helpful for socialization, provided it's the right class conducted by a knowledgeable instructor. Some teachers allow rough play between large and small dogs. This can not only injure your puppy but it can be a setback to his confidence around other dogs. Some trainers offer classes for small dogs only, and this option is often preferable to all-breed classes. However, don't avoid big dogs altogether. With the right trainer's help, you want your Chi to learn about bigger dogs so he doesn't run from them, thereby causing the big dog to see him as prey and give chase. Socialization must be done with care. When you allow playtime with bigger dogs, make sure they are unflappable and calm around small dogs. Supervise this play time to make sure your Chihuahua is treated with respect by older dogs.

CRATE TRAINING

Crate training your Chi puppy is useful for housetraining, confinement—and your sanity. Crate training allows you to leave your home knowing that, when you return, your puppy will be safe and nothing will be chewed up or soiled. Confining your pup in a crate may save his life—puppies have been known to chew through electrical cords and many other unsafe household items when left unsupervised.

Crates have been given a bad rap by some uniformed dog lovers. They think it's wrong to confine a dog. In fact, the opposite is true—it's cruel not to give a dog a space of his own. The crate is a sanctuary for your dog, much like a den would be for the wild canine. It is your Chi's own private bedroom, where he can retire when tired, but still be part of family life.

HOW TO CRATE TRAIN

How you crate train your dog will determine whether he accepts a crate or fights the process. Many good breeders will have started crate training before you bring your puppy home. To continue the training (or if your Chi is not used to being confined), start feeding him his meals in his crate. Lure him in with toys, treats, and chews, and leave the crate door open until he gets used to coming and going. Put the crate next to your bed before you call it a day and encourage him to sleep there. When he's used to the open crate, start closing the crate door for a few seconds with him inside. If he doesn't fuss, let him out and praise him. Then throw some more treats inside and keep the door shut for longer periods of time.

The key to making this work is to never let the pup out when he's whining. Instead, wait for the moment when he stops to catch his breath and reward that silence by immediately letting him out and praising him. Playing with you will be his reward for being calm and quiet in the crate.

HOUSETRAINING

Toy dogs are legendary for being harder to housetrain than large dogs, and Chihuahuas are no exception. One reason may be that it's much easier to overlook the tiny puddles small dogs leave behind, because they are just droplets that disappear rapidly into the carpet. By the time your little one has emptied his bladder, the wet spot may disappear, but unfortunately the smell will be apparent to your dog. And if he can smell it, he'll think that it's okay to relieve himself there again and again.

Another problem is the Chihuahua's tiny bladder. It needs to be emptied frequently. What may seem to you like a short time since your Chi went potty may seem like an eternity to him. If he's not given enough chances to potty outside, he's bound to have more accidents. The more accidents your puppy makes, the more ingrained this bad habit becomes, and the harder it will be to correct and housetrain your puppy.

However, with the right combination of vigilance, patience, and time, you can housetrain your Chihuahua. Choosing an appropriate method to teach your Chi will help the process along. It is easier to teach your Chi where you would like him to eliminate, than scolding him for going where you don't want.

HOW TO HOUSETRAIN

Choose a word or phrase that you'll use to associate with the act: "hurry up," "go to it!" or simply "potty" are all fine choices. Take your Chihuahua puppy outside to his designated potty spot and say the word. Be sure to stand and wait for him to figure out what to do when you say "potty" (or whatever word you've chosen). As soon as your puppy goes, make sure he knows he did the right thing by praising him and offering him a treat. Bring the puppy in after treating him.

If you housetrain your Chihuahua in this way, he will associate the reward with the act. By rewarding him for going in his spot, he'll learn much faster than just letting him out by himself. After all, if he's outside on his own, how can you expect your puppy to read your mind that he's outside for a purpose and not just to explore? Plus, putting the act on a cue like this can come in handy when you are traveling or your schedule changes.

Some people choose to use a litterbox or turf box (you may live in a high-rise apartment or have trouble getting outdoors quickly). If you choose this method, the housetraining rules are the same, except that you take the pup to the litterbox instead of outside. One advantage of litterbox training is that you can leave it out when you can't get home to let the dog outside.

Take Him Out Often

The idea is get your puppy out as frequently as possible. He will need to go potty first thing in the morning, after eating, after playing, after naps—and many times in between! A good rule of thumb is to set up a regular schedule of taking him out every hour, and then anytime you notice signs that he needs to potty. These signals include circling and sniffing the floor. However, some pups give very little indication that they need to go—they just pause in the middle of whatever they are doing to potty—then bang! They're off and running again.

Supervision and Containment

Bladder control is dictated by biology; impulse control will come with time and training. Therefore, the best way to forestall accidents is total supervision when you're home and containment when you aren't able to watch the pup.

Using a crate for housetraining can be helpful because it's in a dog's nature to keep his den area (the crate) and himself clean. When you can't be there to supervise your puppy, confine him to a crate. As a *general* rule of thumb, a puppy can hold his bladder for the number of hours equal to his age in months plus one. For example, if the pup is 3 months old, he can hold his bladder for 4 hours; if he is 4 months, he can hold it for 5 hours. No dog, even an adult, should be asked to hold it more than 7 or 8 hours. Although this generalized rule can help a bit, be aware that Chihuahuas don't develop the same capacity to "hold it" as other dogs, because small dog bladders are slower to fully develop that ability. If you find your Chihuahua is having problems, adjust your timetable to accommodate your dog's development. Or, if you are leaving for more time than he can be expected to hold his bladder, then use a small ex-pen with papers at one end and a bed at the other end. This allows the pup to move away from his sleeping

It may take a bit of time, but you can housetrain your little dog.

area to eliminate and teaches him that there is a right area to go and to keep things clean.

Puppies can hold it longer at night than during the day when they are more active. While your puppy is being housetrained, put his crate in the living area, and at night, move the crate to your bedroom—he will feel secure there. It's easy to mistake whining in his crate for wanting to go potty, so until the pup is older, take him out early in the morning and late in the evening before bed.

Consistency

Consistency will bring success—it just may take longer than you had expected to housetrain your little

Don't punish your Chi for housetraining mistakes.

dog. This whole process seems labor intensive, but it will make the difference in your dog's long-term ability to learn to control his bladder.

DEALING WITH ACCIDENTS

Clean up any accidents with an enzymatic cleaning product made especially for dogs. It will remove all traces of the odor that keeps your pup coming back to the same area to eliminate. Also, don't punish your Chihuahua if he has an accident—it will only encourage him to seek places out of your sight to relieve himself. This leads to the accidents going unnoticed by you and will reinforce in the dog's mind that it is okay to potty indoors as long as no one sees him.

BASIC TRAINING

Basic training is about teaching your Chihuahua the minimum he'll need to be a good pet. Training also teaches your puppy to look to you for direction and guidance. The quality time spent with your Chi builds a bond between you—your relationship with your Chihuahua is essentially the cornerstone of training.

Generally, when training a dog, remember these tips:

- When he performs the command consistently, start rewarding the dog *intermittently*. For example, once he understands the down command, start giving him his treat after the second correct down. Then, the next time, give him a reward on every third response. Mix it up so he doesn't know when he gets the treat.
- After treating him intermittently, you can start *fading* the treats. This means to stop giving treats and use only praise. However, I recommend you never totally fade the treats. Instead, continue intermittent treating with longer and longer spaces between treats so the dog never knows for sure when it's coming. Before you start fading out rewards, be sure that the behavior is fully generalized, which means your dog will perform the behavior absolutely, not just in isolated places or conditions.
- The easier and more established the behavior, the less you need to reward/treat the dog. The harder the behavior (new behavior? new environment? more distractions?), the higher the rate of reinforcement (reward/treat) should be.

Train your puppy indoors until he's ready for additional distractions.

WHAT'S HIS STYLE?

Understanding your Chihuahua will help you determine his training style. Some Chis have great energy and want to interact with you; these dogs can be trained for longer periods of time. Some Chis have a more easygoing style, and if you push them too long, they will rebel; these Chihuahuas need breaks from training regularly.

However, even if your Chi seems more than willing, still keep training sessions relatively short. A 5- to 8-minute lesson once or twice a day is sufficient. Try to end each training session on a good note. Don't drill the dog, or he won't understand what behavior you're asking for. When he understands the lesson, end it.

Then reward your Chi with a bit of play or
a walk.

WHERE SHOULD YOU TRAIN?

Start lessons indoors until your pup reliably knows the
commands. Then move your lessons to a small outdoor
fenced-in area. When your puppy performs well in this
area, start adding distractions, such as kids walking by
the outside of the fence. When he works well with
distractions, move to larger, safe areas to retrain the
same commands. Don't be surprised if your Chi-Chi acts
as if he doesn't know the commands when distractions
and new locations are used. This is normal—he needs
to learn that what you want from him applies in all situations. You may need to start
from the beginning when training in a new location.

BE AWARE!
Play can be a great
training reward, but you
might want to think twice
about playing tug of
war. This may not be the
best game to play with
Chihuahuas because their
teeth aren't as strong as
those of other breeds.

WHAT TYPE OF REWARDS?

Both food and play can be used as rewards in training.
- **Food:** The treats should be small; use dog biscuits, tiny bits of chicken or beef,
  or anything your Chi likes to eat; make sure it's a tiny bit each time you treat so
  he doesn't get full or overweight.
- **Play:** You can use play or other significant activities (like walking together) as a
  reward. Most canines find playtime and walking a "high-value" activity, and these
  can be used to reward any desired behavior. Dogs who are not food motivated
  can often be trained knowing that the reward will be his favorite activity.

WHAT IF HE MAKES A MISTAKE?

If you don't get the correct response during training, don't yell "bad dog" or
"no"—that is counterproductive. Try saying "uh oh" or "whoops" in a calm voice
to let him know that's not the behavior you wanted. Then wait until you can lure
him into whatever command you're working on (e.g., *down* or *sit*). You also don't
want to use physical corrections. Physical corrections are counterproductive—
your Chi will try to avoid the lesson and not be eager to learn or be around you.

BASIC COMMANDS

Now it's time to grab some treats to start the games. If you think of training as a
fun activity to do with your Chi rather than drudgery, it will take you a long way
toward getting your dog's cooperation.

Here are six basic behaviors that every dog should learn.

WATCH ME

Concentration, if that's what you think your Chihuahua lacks, comes from training. Getting and keeping your Chihuahua's attention through eye contact is the basis for communicating with your dog and teaching him all other commands. Therefore, the *watch me* (or *focus*) command should be taught before the rest of training begins. It's similar to teaching young children—in order to teach them, they need to be quiet and listening. How do you know you have their attention? They're looking at you.

- Start by giving your dog a treat and then showing him another treat in your other hand.
- Hold the treat up to your eyes.
- When the dog glances at you, toss him the treat.
- After a few tries, it won't take him long to look at you.
- Next, ask that he watches you for more than a moment before you toss the treat to him.
- Finally, attach the cue word to the action. Say "watch me," and when he looks at you, toss the treat.

Teaching the *sit* is fairly easy.

Luring a dog into a down can be more difficult than a sit because down is a more vulnerable position.

Once you have taught him to focus on you, then you can start to train him in other lessons. When you ask your Chi to do something, make sure he gives you eye contact before moving on.

SIT

Teaching your Chihuahua to sit is fairly easy because it's something he does naturally. To teach the *sit*:

- Show your Chi a treat and then hold it just above his nose.
- Slowly move the treat over your Chi's head—between his ears toward his bottom.
- Most dogs will naturally sit by following the treat with their nose.
- When his rear hits the floor, even if momentarily, give him the treat and lots of praise—tell him what a good dog he is!
- When your puppy starts to understand the command, add the cue word. Say, "sit" then show the reward.
- When the dog complies, praise and reward

Don't ever push him down physically. This creates resistance in the dog and doesn't produce the willing team attitude you want.

DOWN

Luring a dog into a *down* can be more difficult than a *sit* because down is a more vulnerable position.

- Have your Chi sit.
- Hold a treat in front of his nose, then slowly move it down to the floor.
- If he follows it down to the ground, reward him with the treat.
- If he stops part way down, then reward small movements into the down position and keep praising and treating until he goes all the way down.
- Once you have your Chi in the down position, give him a "jackpot," which means rapidly giving him multiple treats for staying down.
- As training progresses and the puppy begins to understand *down*, add the command by saying "down," then showing the reward.
- When he complies, praise and reward.

Down is a great command to train. If your Chi is a bit excited, the action of lying down and staying in that position will help calm him.

STAY

To teach the *stay* command:
- Start with your hands full of treats.
- Ask your Chihuahua to sit (you can also use the *down* position).
- Feed him one treat at a time in rapid succession as long as he remains in position—this rewards the dog as he stays.
- Stop the rewards when you are ready to release the dog from the *stay*.
- Say "okay" (or something similar) as your release word, and allow the dog to get up; this will increase the Chi's interest in doing this exercise and he will want to stay put until you end the exercise.
- If your Chi gets up before hearing the release word, he stops getting the treats.
- Don't say anything, just put him back in position and restart the lesson.
- When your Chi is good at staying, take a step away; then return and reward the stay with the treat.
- Once he's got that down, take two steps away.
- Keeping increasing the distance as he gets more reliable.
- Remember to say "okay" or "finished" when finished; the release word tells him there is no more reward for staying.

The stay command will come in handy in a lot of situations, such as when you are at the vet's office and need to weigh him.

COME

Come is the *most important lesson* you must teach your dog. I can't stress this enough. The Chihuahua is vulnerable and so clever that it takes only a small slip up before he's streaking out the front door and into traffic. When your Chi instantly responds to the *come* command, you will know you can keep him safe.

Chihuahuas want to think they are in charge of every situation, so getting this breed to come to you can be challenging. Therefore, teaching *come* (or *here*) must be a joyful, cheery event. Always call him in a happy voice to teach him it's a wonderful, exciting thing to run to you.

Never, ever, ever use *come* to punish the dog. Don't immediately leash him or end the play, or he will associate the word *come* with bad news. You need him to be *delighted* to come to you, or you will teach him the opposite—running from you when ask for him to come. After all, your Chihuahua isn't stupid; would you willingly run to someone who you think is going to "chew you out" or lock you up?

Puppyhood is the best time to start training this command, because when he's a baby he will want to be with you and will naturally follow you. You can take the opportunity to add a "come" (or a "here") when he's following you, and then play with him or treat him when he arrives. This way, you can turn the cue into an automatic response. When he becomes excited by the word "come" and comes to you eagerly, you can start more formal training.

To teach *come*:

• In a securely fenced-in area, run a few feet (m) away from your dog and sing out

Once your Chi has a reliable *come* in a fenced-in area, practice in other places with a long line or leash attached to his collar.

"come" in a happy voice.
- Your pup's natural response will be to chase you.
- Repeat the steps above, gradually increasing the distance you run away from him.
- When you have a reliable recall in the fenced area, attach a 10- to 20-foot (3- to 6-m) light line to your Chi's collar.
- Go into areas and situations with increasing distractions and ask him to come.
- Use the light line to gently reel him in if he balks (never jerk on the line) and continue to praise him so he makes the connection that not coming isn't an option.

If your Chi has difficulty coming immediately around distractions, go back to an area where there are fewer distractions to practice. Make yourself more interesting by playing with the pup and treating him every time he does the right thing. You can then start fading the reward to every other time, then treat randomly before you fade the reward totally.

HEEL

The *heel* command is used to keep your dog next to you on walks so that you can move together in unison. Use a collar and leash—never a choke chain. Also, never tug on your Chi's delicate neck with the leash, as this could hurt him. While a harness can be fine for informal walks, I would stick to a soft collar and leash for *heel*, especially if you are going to go on to do obedience or classes of any kind.

To teach *heel*:
- Start out by saying "heel" (or "let's go").
- Start out with your left leg, and walk while patting your leg in an inviting way.
- You can try putting a treat in front of his nose while you're walking. (Since you'll need to bend down, this can be difficult for long periods of time.)
- Once he walks a few steps with you, praise him and treat.
- If he pulls on the leash, change directions and soon he'll be walking with you.

CHAPTER 8

SOLVING PROBLEMS
WITH YOUR
CHIHUAHUA

He can be tough, willful, and self-assured—yes, I'm talking about your Chihuahua. Physically, he isn't a large dog, but in his mind he believes he can take on that German Shepherd Dog down the street. Chihuahuas have enough chutzpah to think that by sheer power of will they can get their own way—and they usually do. This can lead to problems for you and your dog.

In any group of living beings, there must be standards of behavior for the safety of all in the group. Order is a fact of life in all social groups—and that includes the family dog, who wants to live in harmony and not turmoil. If you teach your Chihuahua the rules of behavior as a young puppy, he should continue on his path to good citizenship. Solid, positive training means your dog has learned self-control in situations that require it.

However, even with the best of intentions, problem behaviors can occur with your Chi that need to be addressed before they spiral out of control.

WHAT IS A PROBLEM BEHAVIOR?

Your Chihuahua stands on his hind legs and nonstop barks at anything that moves outside of the picture window; sometimes, he barks endlessly at nothing that moves. Your Chihuahua nips at a visiting friend while sitting on your couch. Your Chihuahua goes potty all over the house; you can't seem to get him to stop.

Even though your Chihuahua is small, an aggressive dog of any size is a problem.

I found that if I didn't train my Chi, Celia, a few minutes every day when she was learning something new, she would pretend that she'd forgotten it. Once I started training her every day, she's much more likely to remember what I've been teaching her. Plus, it's quality time spent with her, and it's done wonders to build up her confidence.

Does any of this sound familiar? These are all problem behaviors that Chihuahua owners may have to face at some point. Problem behaviors are behaviors that work against the harmony of owning a dog. While not all of them are dangerous, any problem that disrupts the family or social network needs to be dealt with, or the dog risks isolation and worse—abandonment. Many problem behaviors are intentionally or unintentionally encouraged. For example, when Charm was a Chi puppy and she growled, her family thought it was cute because of the incongruity between the fierceness of the growl and her teeny body. Everybody laughed and gave her affection whenever she growled, which in her mind was a reward for the behavior of growling. Now, as an adult, she has graduated to not only growling at but biting her owners. Suddenly, the behavior is not so cute anymore.

If you are faced with a problem behavior, check that your dog management skills aren't at fault, and you aren't unwittingly encouraging the problem. Also make sure your dog is getting enough social time, attention, and exercise, since the root of some problems is boredom or lack of socialization. Try channeling your Chi's energy into something that's constructive. For example, redirect chewing on your rugs to chewing on a rope-toy.

Keep things in perspective as you work with your Chihuahua; realize that most problems are fixable and that if you're willing to put in the time, you can get past it. The love and laughter you get from your dog outweighs the issues that need to be corrected. With any recurring or persistent behavior problem, it is always best to seek advice from your vet because behavior problems may be the result of medical issues.

AGGRESSION

In 2008, *The Journal of Applied Animal Science* published a compiled report that discussed aggression in dogs. The study listed the top dog breeds most likely to bite—and Chihuahuas are on that list! Lack of training and proper socialization were the most likely culprits.

Even though your Chihuahua is small, a biting dog of any size is a problem. What was cute as a puppy isn't so cute when a Chihuahua bites someone's face as they lean down to pet him. Not only is it dangerous, but you will probably lose friends if your dog's biting is tolerated by you. A dog who has been known to bite one person will generally keep it in his repertoire for the next time, and the next, until the problem is solved. If it is reported to the authorities, your Chihuahua can have a record just like any other criminal—and that is no laughing matter.

The first thing you should do is take your Chihuahua to the veterinarian to make sure he's not suffering from a physical cause for aggression. After he's cleared, think about management and training.

While there are many types of aggression, aggressive Chihuahuas are usually fearful Chihuahuas. Their minds go into an "I must bite first, if not I'll be hurt" mindset. Fear will drive your Chi's aggression, and it will eventually become a habit if not addressed.

Your Chi needs to know that you are his leader and will keep him safe. If not, he will act aggressively when faced with what he sees as a threat. The best way to build your Chi's confidence in you (and himself) is through training. Obedience training and training for a sport like agility can do wonders for a Chi's confidence.

If your Chihuahua's aggression continues, it's time to find a professional. Find a dog behaviorist who knows how to work with aggressive dogs. Do not avoid this problem and hope it goes away—you must get help before it escalates.

BARKING

Chihuahuas have a reputation for barking a lot, and it's a well-earned title. Toy dogs in general are a noisy bunch. It can become an annoying problem that feeds on itself, and is often the reason some Chis are locked away in isolation or even given up to a shelter. While barking is a perfectly natural behavior for dogs, when it becomes excessive, it's a problem. Excessive barking should be handled early, with prevention and management in order to avoid trying to correct it later on when it's an ingrained habit.

WHY DOGS BARK

Dogs bark for good reasons. To manage the problem, first find out why your Chi is barking excessively.

- Dogs bark to alarm the household that someone is trespassing on the property. (While this is great if it's a burglar, it's not so good when it's your best friend stopping by and your Chi-Chi won't stop woofing while you are trying to catch up on gossip.)

- Dogs generally bark at changes in their surroundings, be it joggers, mailmen, cars passing the house, kids playing, and bicycles riding by the house.
- Dogs bark when they are stressed out or bored.
- Sometimes dogs bark when their owner leaves them at home alone; this can mean the dog has separation anxiety.
- Small dogs tend to bark more than big dogs, and one reason may be their size—everything in their world is giant. To keep danger at bay, they bark to protect themselves.
- You may be unintentionally encouraging your Chihuahua to bark when you ask him "who's at the door?" when someone knocks. Or, if you pet him or pick him up when he barks or talk to him in a babyish soothing voice. That's rewarding to him, and he thinks you approve of the barking.
- Chihuahuas who have not been socialized sufficiently will bark excessively when they meet strangers.

MANAGEMENT

Don't punish your Chihuahua for barking too much. Shouting at your dog just increases his excitement. The way to reduce barking is to ignore the dog when he's barking for your attention and then work on the problem. Don't reward excess barking behavior, reward quietness.

If the barking problem is due to a lack of socialization, exposure to people and noises will reduce the need to bark as your puppy gets older.

If your Chihuahua feels he has to protect himself by barking to keep someone at bay, then you haven't gained his respect. He figures that you can't protect him, so he better do it himself. Train him in a positive manner to earn his respect: ask him to sit before you feed him, have him sit before you allow him outside, don't coddle him when he's afraid. Your Chihuahua needs to know that you are in charge and will take care of him, and he doesn't need to protect himself.

If your Chihuahua is barking when you leave the house, get him used to being alone by putting him in his crate or a separate room for a few minutes while you are home. Gradually increase the time the dog is alone. When you release him from the crate, calmly praise him but don't overdo it. Do this every day (even when you are home) to accustom your Chihuahua to feeling secure when he's alone.

If your Chihuahua is bored or lonely, give him a dog toy that's stuffed with food when he's alone. This can help distract him. Other good distractions include leaving the radio or television on when you're gone. Make sure your Chi gets some exercise and human interaction every day.

Last, teach your dog to speak on command, and then teach the *quiet* command. Arm yourself with some high-value treats like pieces of chicken or beef. You want him to bark, so get him excited and barking at something, or play bark at him. When he barks back say, "speak" and then treat him. Say, "quiet" when he stops, and reward him with a few choice pieces. The next time he barks, praise him for a few barks (this may be the first time you have praised him for barking and may confuse him) then say, "okay, quiet." When he stops barking, praise him and dispense lots of treats. Repeat these steps a few times throughout the day. You have communicated to him that it is fine for him to alert you about something new, but after the first alert he's done his job and should stop.

CHEWING

Like barking, chewing is something dogs do naturally, but It can become a problem when your Chihuahua chews on your belongings.

Chewing is especially normal with puppies, since they like to try out everything with their mouths. Puppies will generally grow out of this behavior, but in the meantime offer substitutes for destructive chewing. Provide him with plenty of suitable chew toys.

Redirect him when he's chewing on the wrong items. Make a trade with him— offer him a yummy chewy for the item that you don't want him to chew. If that doesn't work, distract him by taking a couple of steps away and playing with one of his toys yourself. Make fun noises, and when he comes over to check out the excitement, offer him the chewy you want him to have and take away the forbidden item. If he takes the offer, praise him to let him know that you approve.

Boredom is often a contributing factor in chewing. Don't leave your Chi alone for long periods of time. Find the chew toy that keeps your Chihuahua interested and his mind active. Show it to him, then place it a few feet (m) away and praise him when he takes it. Gradually increase the distance until he is searching for the chewy. This kind of "find it" game can help entertain him, get him interested

Don't leave things around that you don't want your puppy to chew on.

114

in appropriate chew toys, and help eliminate the kind of boredom that leads to destructive behaviors.

Last, prevention is key! Don't leave things around that you don't want your puppy to chew on.

DIGGING

Digging is another natural instinct for a dog. Dogs dig to locate enticing smells and bury bones or other tidbits. Sometimes Chis dig to find and eat roots, worms, and dirt.

Boredom is often the root cause of digging, so you may be leaving your dog alone too long. Exercise and mental stimulation help to reduce or stop digging. If your Chihuahua continues to dig, collect some his feces from the yard or potty pan and place it in the hole. He'll most likely avoid that spot.

Another option is to offer him his own special place to dig—a small part of your yard that's his. How about a sandbox? Mark off a small spot in your yard that you can turn into your Chi's own digging area. Guide him to it, encourage him to dig there, and praise him when he does. Digging is a self-rewarding activity for most dogs, so just directing him to the sandbox often solves the problem.

HOUSE SOILING

Accidents happen. However, it's a problem when your "housetrained" Chi-Chi is constantly having accidents on your floors or on your carpet. Age or medical reasons can be the cause of house soiling, but more than likely the problem lies with improper housetraining.

A QUESTION OF HOUSETRAINING

House soiling is often the result of the dog not understanding that he needs to go to the correct potty area. Usually it's a case of mismanagement from not

thoroughly teaching the dog to begin with. If you are having problems
ask yourself:

- Have you supervised the puppy constantly?
- Have you been consistently showing the pup where he's supposed to go?
- Has your Chi been to the veterinarian to see if he's physically able to hold it and that he has no medical issues?
- Have you rewarded your dog enough when he eliminates in the designated potty spot?
- How long has your Chi had the habit? (If it's been a long time, it will be harder to fix.)

It's time to go back to housetraining 101.

Take Time

If your Chi's housetraining was not carried out correctly and for a long enough time, you will need to start from scratch. (Re-read the "Housetraining" section of Chapter 7 to remind yourself of all the steps.) If he's house soiling, he has not learned the correct habit. Realize that, with housetraining, all good things take time. When it comes to housetraining, the more time spent teaching and supervising your dog the better.

To make potty time more predictable for you, schedule feeding and potty times. Doing so gets your dog into a rhythm that he can predict and teaches him to hold it until then. You may need to take him out every hour in the beginning. And you will have to stay with him until he eliminates in the proper spot in order to reward him. This is so he knows he's done the "right thing." If you give up and take him in before he goes, he'll learn that it's okay to go outside and then come back inside and potty. If you do need to come in before he goes, confine him in a small pen with a bed at one end and newspapers on every inch of floor space (or use a litterbox).

Be persistent and consistent in your housetraining efforts, and you will have success.

Clean Up for Success

If you didn't spend enough time on housetraining your puppy or missed the times your Chi went in the house, his accidents left behind an odor that's like a beacon for him to return to. By not sufficiently cleaning up the scent with an enzymatic cleaner, your dog will be lured back to that area. To solve this problem, use an enzymatic cleaner to thoroughly clean up the areas that your dog has marked. After your puppy is housetrained, call in the carpet cleaning pros and get the entire carpet cleaned; that way, if you've missed a spot this will remove all traces of odor.

IS SUBMISSIVE PEEING THE PROBLEM?

Dogs who urinate when you come home or approach them are submissively peeing. It can also be caused by looming over your Chi, which can make him feel intimidated. In the dog world, one way to show submission is to release a small amount of urine. It's a way to calm the aggressor. If a person is perceived as menacing by a timid dog, he may start peeing as a means of calming the person. This makes total sense in dog world. Understand he is only trying to appease you, so yelling or harsh words will only make the situation worse. Stop any reprimands and start some positive reinforcement.

Walk away from your dog when he becomes submissive and wait for him to approach you. The act of greeting him or bending over him can trigger this response. A better way to approach him is by crouching down to the dog's level, but don't make a move to touch him. Don't say a word, as this may evoke the submissive response again. Wait until he is relaxed before talking to him in a normal tone of voice.

Dogs usually grow out of this stage if it's handled correctly.

IS MARKING THE PROBLEM?

If your housetraining is absolutely solid, but you still find urine in the house, it may be the result of a marking problem. Intact males or females sometimes mark areas with urine. Males lift their legs while females squat while trying to aim. If you have a dog who hasn't been spayed/neutered, it's an uphill battle to go against nature and stop the problem. You must be super diligent about cleaning up any areas where the dog marks.

If your Chi is having accidents in the house, there's a good chance he wasn't properly housetrained to begin with.

AGE COUNTS

How old is your Chi? Is he mature enough to hold his bladder? Is he a senior dog? Older dogs have incontinence problems that can be helped with medication, so see your Chi's vet. Weak bladder control can cause a puppy or young dog to lose control of his bladder upon greeting you. Modify the way you greet your dog when you come home, and make sure to keep your demeanor toned down. Too much excitement at greeting can make a puppy overstimulated and he can leak. Puppies typically grow out of this stage.

JUMPING UP

Jumping up is hard to avoid with Chihuahuas because of their size—

Jumping up is hard to avoid with Chihuahuas because of their size.

it's natural to let them jump up so you don't have to lean down so far. Owners inadvertently train their dogs to jump up by allowing this to happen. However, it becomes a problem when others don't like this attention or when it rips pantyhose or scratches bare legs.

One technique to deal with jumping up is *counter conditioning*. This means teaching your dog a different behavior as an alternative to the one you don't want. This way, he still gets what he wants—attention—but by doing a behavior of your choosing.

An arrival at the door is most likely what starts your Chi-Chi jumping up for a greeting. You should already have taught your dog the *sit*, so arm yourself with treats and walk through the door. Ask your dog to sit. When he sits, treat him and shower him with attention. Start asking your dog to sit before you give him attention, and it will become a habit.

Another option to stop jumping up is to turn your back on the dog when he jumps. Then wait until he calms down and give him a treat. Don't feed him the treat until all four feet are firmly planted on the ground. If your Chi is not treat motivated, you can do the same thing only offer praise and attention when he's on the ground. Teaching the "off" command can then be added. The least confrontational way to teach *off* is to back away from the dog or turn your back to him when he jumps on you, say "off," and then have the dog sit. Praise and treat when the dog makes the correct choice. You shouldn't say "down" when you want your dog to get off of you. That will only confuse him, since you have already taught him that "down" (the *down* command) means lie down.

NIPPING

Nipping is never acceptable behavior. It's the kind of behavior that reinforces itself because it keeps people away. However, nipping can escalate until the dog is biting everyone—family members included. This behavior needs to be modified so it doesn't escalate. As with the problem of aggression, take your Chihuahua to the veterinarian to make sure he's not suffering from a physical cause.

If an adult Chi is nipping, it may be that the behavior wasn't directed appropriately in puppyhood. Littermates quickly and effectively teach each other how hard to bite. If a puppy bites too hard, his littermate will respond by walking away from play or becoming more aggressive to counteract the roughness. Bite inhibition is a powerful social rule that dogs learn to control by play. This is one reason it's better to get your Chihuahua puppy after 8 to 12 weeks of age—his littermates have taught him bite inhibition.

Perhaps you've subtly encouraged the nipping. Your new darling puppy arrives home, and he gives you a nip on the finger as you're playing. But you forgive your cute puppy because, after all, he is just a baby! Never allow play biting; it encourages the puppy to believe it is okay. On the other hand, don't yell at your Chi for nipping because it just makes the game more fun—now he has excitement! And puppies live for excitement.

If your dog nips, walk away and stop any interactions to discourage that behavior. Return after the dog settles down and give him a chance to interact without nipping. With some puppies, saying "ouch" loudly and walking away from him works, but sometimes this technique doesn't get the correct message through. If your puppy is highly reactive, you may scare him. If your pup has the opposite personality, where he decides your exclamation is an invitation to play the "ouch game" and try to bite you more passionately, your ouch may encourage the dog to bite more aggressively. If saying "ouch" doesn't get you the results you want, don't use that technique. Avoid any games that consist of dog teeth on human skin.

If your dog has learned nipping and is not easily discouraged from the activity, do not raise the stakes by using harsh methods on him. It will only be seen by the dog

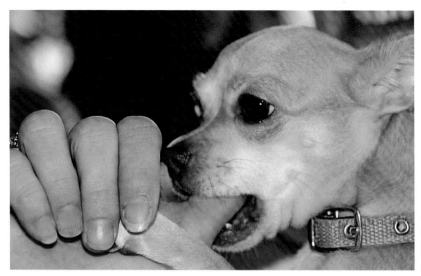

While mouthing is normal behavior in puppies, it should not be encouraged or it may turn to nipping.

as a threat and may have the effect of escalating the nipping. Seek professional help if you are unable to stop your Chi from nipping. Never allow nipping behavior to continue because it won't improve on its own, it will only get worse.

WHEN TO SEEK PROFESSIONAL HELP

A dog who has sudden changes in his behavior is a cause for concern. Sometimes behavior changes are due to normal circumstances and can be simple to remedy. A change in your household, such as a new member of the family or someone moving out, can disturb your Chi, and he may just need some time to adjust. If you are spending less time with your dog for any reason, think about sending him to dog daycare or making doggy playdates so he can interact with other dogs. Chihuahuas are sensitive to being left alone. If your pup is under 1 to 2 years of age, he may not have reached maturity yet, and he just needs consistency in training until he grows up.

However, sometimes it's not easy to define why a behavior has changed. The first thing to do is visit your veterinarian to make sure there are no medical reasons for problem behaviors.

When you see aggression in any dog, seek out a professional to help you through the problem. A Chihuahua may be less likely to seriously hurt someone by biting them, but he can get himself hurt if he challenges the wrong dog or person. And children, who are often on the same level as your Chi, may get bitten on the face.

If your Chihuahua bites someone, you need to find a professional trainer. As soon as your Chi learns that using aggression gets him what he's after, he may always see this option as a way of getting what he wants. Other aggressive problems can include fighting with other dogs and resource guarding, and a trainer or behaviorist can help you to deal with these problems. They can teach your dog management techniques after getting your Chi under control.

PUPPY POINTER

Pamper your puppy without spoiling him. Lay down and stick to the rules that you want your dog to keep before he's an adult, and devise other ways to indulge him. You don't need to eliminate affection and treats. Don't hesitate to dish them out for good behaviors—especially yummy treats when your Chihuahua has been good. Other great indulgences include a visit with other toy dogs to play or a little play time with a toy.

Problem behaviors like barking or jumping up can be hard to control, even by experienced dog owners. If your Chi exhibits any issue you can't solve—it's time to find a professional. A trainer or behaviorist will evaluate your individual problems, and it may only take a simple change to teach your dog the right behavior.

FINDING A BEHAVIORIST

Dog trainers and behaviorists are not a regulated field, so be cautious when selecting one. The exception is veterinary behaviorists, who are veterinarians with advanced education in the field of animal behavior. Most owners will probably look for a dog trainer for help, but not all trainers specialize in behavioral problems.

It is up to you to decide whether the person you use is qualified. Ask your veterinarian if she knows of a specialist in dog behavior. Also check if your local shelter has a list of good behaviorists and trainers.

Ask if the trainer or behaviorist has had experience with your dog's particular problem. Never choose someone who uses force with dogs to make them comply—look for someone who uses positive training. Go and watch the trainer at her facility as she trains other dogs. Check that the dogs are happy and like their trainer. You can watch quietly and see how the dogs react.

When looking for help, look for these acronyms:
• ACVB: American College of Veterinary Behaviorists
• APDT: The Association of Professional Dog Trainers
• CPDT-KA: Certified Professional Dog Trainer-Knowledge Assessed
• CDBC: Certified Dog Behavior Consultant
• IAABC: International Association of Animal Behavior Consultants

ACTIVITIES WITH YOUR CHIHUAHUA

The public's perception of Chihuahuas as fashion statements stashed in a handbag whose paws never touch the ground is woefully wrong. Sure, he loves to go out on the town with you, but there is more to this little dynamo than that. You'll find your Chi eager for sports, training, and just plain time off the sofa and out of the house to get some of that sunshine he craves so much.

Chihuahuas have an intrinsic need to run around on the ground, just like any other breed of dog. They are athletic and lively and want to do something with all that energy. Plus, exercising with your dog has the added benefit of helping both you and your Chihuahua stay fit and healthy.

Chihuahuas may be considered lapdogs, but don't just offer your lap to your dog. Consider dog sports and canine activities that will get you two up off the sofa and into life! Many Chihuahuas can be competitive athletes if allowed the opportunity.

SPORTS AND ACTIVITIES

Some Chi owners enjoy casual activities like going for a walk or throwing a ball, while other people like to explore their competitive side and try out performance or show ring events.

ACTIVITIES (NON-COMPETITIVE)

Chihuahuas only need moderate exercise, but it's a good idea to plan on doing some kind of activity every day with your dog. That activity can be as simple as taking a walk. If you have a yard, allowing him outside can provide a little activity, but with most Chihuahuas, you'll need to do a little more. Most Chis left on their own outside will sniff around a few seconds and then want to be let back in with you.

Some owners find hiking with their Chis is great fun. It's important to bring a dog backpack if you hike a lot because your mile (2 km) of easy hiking is equivalent to about 40 miles (64 km) to the Chihuahua. You'll need to carry him for part of the hike if you are a marathon hiker. The Chihuahua is never one to turn down a ride, so putting him into your backpack while you continue on is enjoyable to him after he tires.

AGILITY

Agility is a fast-moving, exciting sport. In this timed event, your Chi competes against other dogs in a doggy obstacle course. The handler guides the dog through hoops, on a teeter-totter, over jumps, and through tunnels. Dogs may navigate through weave poles and along a balance beam. The handler typically runs alongside or nearby the dog. Spectators and family sit outside the ring to cheer you and your Chi along.

Agility is offered by several organizations in the United States, including the American Kennel Club (AKC). Nowadays, you don't need a registered dog to do agility at an AKC show, but you do need to register with the AKC's Canine Partner's program. Two other major agility organizations are the United States Dog Agility Association (USDAA) and North American Dog Agility Association (NADAA). These organizations offer agility to all dogs regardless of their breed.

The best way to get started in this sport is to enroll in an agility class where dog and handler learn how to conquer the obstacles and refine their teamwork.

TDAA Agility

A newcomer agility organization is the Teacup Dog Agility Association (TDAA), which offers competition only to small dogs. According to the TDAA, "The purpose of the Teacup Dogs Agility Association is to provide a competitive venue for dogs of small stature without regard to breed or pedigree." Because agility is designed for larger dogs, it makes it difficult for some toys to participate. Some of the problems a Chihuahua faces in traditional agility include:

• The height of the grass on the course. Judges complain that they can't see their tiny feet hit the zones because their paws are so small!

• Large dogs are not always under control, and sometimes see a Chi as prey; there is the possibility of injury to toy dogs.

• There can be prejudice against the little guys. Some competitors don't consider them "real" dogs. They don't think they should be allowed to compete and are an inconvenience for the other dogs. Getting more Chis involved in agility is likely to change that perception.

The TDAA was formed to provide a safe place for petite dogs to compete, with obstacles that are scaled down to a size more suitable to smaller dogs like the Chihuahua. Board member and agility judge Cheryl Huffman says, "We definitely have lots of Chis throughout the U.S. that participate in all kinds of agility

Agility is a fast-moving, exciting sport.

including TDAA. Equipment is smaller and distance between obstacles much smaller than traditional agility."

The first TDAA trial was in May 2002. In the first trial, there were about 32 dogs. Now, there are over 1,900 dogs in the TDAA, representing 81 breeds. These trials are reputed to be more casual than the average agility trial. Participation is limited to dogs 17 inches (43 cm) and under, with jumps set in a range from 4 to 16 inches (10 to 41 cm). There's no restriction on breed, type, or pedigree.

TDAA President Bud Houston says:

"What strikes most people first about a TDAA trial is the miniature size of the obstacles. 'Cute' is the word that most often comes to lips. When the exhibitors walk the course they notice the short distances between obstacles. When the teacup dogs hit the course running it's not only cute, it's fast. The small dog is hitting obstacles at about the same pace a Border Collie might work at obstacles set at 15 to 18 feet apart. The epic running between obstacles a small dog handler has to do in a big dog agility event doesn't apply to TDAA classes. That means the handler has to be smart in timing and good on his feet.

Courses and equipment in the other organizations are scaled for the big dogs. Running a Chihuahua on a course intended for a much larger Border Collie is just about as appropriate as running that same big dog on an equestrian cross-country course. TDAA believes agility is not about fast dogs;

they contend that agility is a recreational sport for the family dog. And they believe the little dog will have his day."

CANINE GOOD CITIZEN

The AKC sponsors a program called the Canine Good Citizen Program (CGC) for dogs who have good manners at home and in the community. The CGC test is available to unregistered as well as registered dogs who pass a ten-step assessment and receive a certificate. The best way to prepare for the test is to take the class to train your Chihuahua for it.

Good behavior is judged on several issues, such as how the dog responds to the owner, and how the dog reacts to other dogs and strangers. Other activities, such as therapy dog programs, often require a dog to have a CGC before he can participate. Even if you decide not to take the test with your dog, a CGC class is still a great idea because it makes your Chi a better companion.

K9 NOSE WORK/FUN NOSE WORK

K9 Nose Work or Fun Nose Work is a growing sport that is gaining in popularity among dog owners. This is an activity that anybody, anywhere, with any breed of dog can do at home or in competitions. Even your tiny Chihuahua can do Nose Work, and the great thing about it is that you can do it in the comfort of your own home. You don't even need a class to start doing it, since this is an activity that taps into your Chi's natural instinct to sniff. Plus, it satisfies his need for physical and mental stimulation.

The sport was developed in 2006 by professional trainers of working certified detection dogs, who detect narcotics and explosives. These professional dogs were always happy and relaxed after a search, so the handlers thought companion dogs might enjoy a similar game that didn't require a large space or special equipment.

The objective is for the dog to detect a hidden scented object and to signal the owner of its exact location. In the beginning, the dog is encouraged to find a toy hidden in a box. Later, the toy will be hidden in more unusual places. When the dog becomes more proficient, the object is hidden in more difficult locations, such as inside a box among a group of different boxes, or in a different room so that the dog must search through the house.

It's an ideal activity for Chihuahuas and owners who need a less physically demanding sport. Plus, if you decide to find a competition or play in a park with other owners, Nose Work can help Chis who are shy and reactive around people and other dogs.

Fun Nose Work takes advantage of your Chi's keen sense of smell.

New trainers and instructors are being certified all the time. Check out the National Association of Canine Scent Work (NACSW) for more information.

OBEDIENCE

Owners who want to build and demonstrate a working relationship with their dog might want to try obedience training and competition. Obedience expertise shows off a dog's usefulness and the human and dog team's skill. To do well in obedience competition takes quite a bit of training, but owners say it is a rewarding experience.

In the obedience ring, teams are judged as they execute a series of required exercises. Obedience trials have several levels of complexity. The beginning levels are divided into novice and subnovice. These are essentially the same class, however, all of subnovice is conducted on a leash while portions of novice is conducted off-leash. The class covers the dog heeling on your left side and sitting automatically when you stop walking. The dog will need to stand on command, without moving, at the end of the lead while a judge inspects him. Dogs do 3-minute down-stays and 1-minute sit-stays. The dog will need to come when called and perform a stay in both the sit and down position. Points earned can be applied toward a title.

Linda Cumming's Chihuahua Rosie earned the obedience titles Companion Dog (CD) and Companion Dog Excellent (CDX), then got her Utility Dog (UD) title in February 2009. She was the first Chihuahua to earn her UD; it was not until 3 years after Rosie got her UD that another Chihuahua earned one. Linda was going to retire Rosie after she earned her UD, but Linda's friends encouraged her to go for a Utility Dog Excellent (UDX) title because no Chihuahua has ever earned it. And now the team is on a quest for a UDX.

Rosie has five legs of her UDX—more than any other Chihuahua has ever accomplished. She is the first Chihuahua to get a Versatility title. Linda says she is looking forward to taking her to the Chihuahua Nationals in Chicago to compete with other Chis.

Open level obedience expects the dog not only to heel off-leash but to sit when the handler stops, and do 5-minute downs and sit-stays; the dog needs to retrieve a dumbbell over a jump and do a broad jump on command, and these exercises are all performed off-leash. As with novice obedience, you can accumulate points to earn titles. At the utility level, the dog must display the ability to do retrieving commands as well as discriminate scent.

Dogs can win titles such as:
• CD (Companion Dog)
• CDX (Companion Dog Excellent)
• UD (Utility Dog)
• UDX (Utility Dog Excellent)

Once your dog gets his Utility titles, you can go on to the Versatile Companion titles, which include agility and tracking.

Don't Underestimate Your Chi

Obedience trials aren't just for German Shepherds and Golden Retrievers. Although obedience is among the most challenging sport for any dog, toy dogs do wonderfully in these events. The classes require control and unparalleled communication with your Chi. Watching a little Chihuahua do a *sit-stay* and coming when called is thrilling. So, if you've never considered training your Chihuahua because of their reputation for stubbornness, consider Linda Cumming's story. She has a top-titled AKC Obedience Chihuahua, and had never trained a dog before she started with Rosie.

Linda and her Chihuahua Rosie (Linda's Rosita Bonita UD, VER, RA) live in Tallahassee, Florida and compete in obedience together. Linda has had Chihuahuas for about 15 years, but Rosie is the first dog she's ever trained for obedience. Rosie has earned many AKC Obedience titles and is certified for pet therapy through the Delta Society. Linda never considered entering any class with her Chihuahua until her veterinarian's technician told her Rosie was smart, energetic, and with her wonderful temperament, she thought Rosie would be a great little competitor. Linda started with training classes and was surprised by how much Rosie enjoyed it. Linda said that Rosie is a happy little worker, and she's an incredible Chihuahua.

Having a successful show dog depends mostly on his breeding.

Don't think that this team is the exception—Linda says she has assisted in obedience training for other Chihuahuas, and that many Chihuahuas are capable of learning and excelling at obedience. Many Chis can earn a companion dog title (CD) with some training. Increasing in difficulty is the advanced companion dog excellent title (CDX) and then the utility dog (UD) obedience title.

SHOWING (CONFORMATION)

Conformation dog shows are big crowd pleasers—several AKC shows on the circuit are televised on Animal Planet and other TV stations each year. The Westminster dog show at Madison Square Garden in New York hosts hundreds of the best dogs in the world, competing each year for the prestigious and coveted Best in Show trophy. The big banana in England is the Crufts dog show, which usually has more entries than the Westminster show! However, the time spent in the spotlight of the ring is brief compared to the time spent making it there. Even getting to a local dog show (far below the heights of Westminster) takes lots of time and energy.

What exactly is conformation? It is a show in which breeders send their potential breeding dogs to be judged on how closely they come to the written standard for each breed. After making it to the group rings, the winners move on to the Best of Show ring.

Only one dog out of hundreds at every show will win the sought-after Best in Show (BIS) award. Dog shows are a process of elimination. So, to get to that BIS class, dogs must win other classes to get a chance to compete against other group top dogs for the BIS award. The competition begins at the breed level. Chihuahuas (who are in the Toy Group) compete against other Chihuahuas in the breed classes. The judges choose the best Chihuahua out of the Chihuahua breed classes. This best Chihuahua goes on to compete against the best of the other Toy group breeds (Maltese, Pekingese, etc.). Only the Best of Breed winners advance to compete in the group competitions. All the groups have one representative as best of that group, and these seven dogs finally compete for Best of Show.

The story of getting to any dog show is told in the years before it happens— when breeders plan breedings between their dogs based on many factors, such as genetics and how it relates to structure, movement, pedigree, and health. Breeding a good specimen of a show dog requires time and frequently lots of money. If you are interested in showing, you'll need to buy a really good dog and either handle him yourself or hire a professional handler.

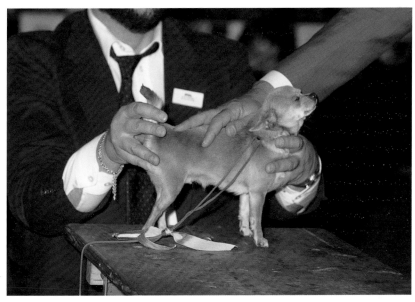

Showing your Chi takes a lot of time and money.

Buying a show dog can be risky business. Out of a litter of puppies, the breeder will consider it a success if she gets one pup who grows into a dog good enough to be shown. The breeder can take an educated guess on the best show-quality puppy, but lots of dogs from perfect bloodlines often don't make the cut. Genetics is an inexact science—it's much more like an art.

If you go this route, expect hard work and lots of good times with animals you love and people who share that feeling. If you want to be part of the excitement, then conformation is for you. If you'd rather not strut your stuff against the very stiff competition of the bluebloods, there are other classes you can participate in that are more casual (but no less competitive).

Check the AKC's website (www.akc.org) to get more information on purebreds and how to find a local club where you can take classes. Local clubs often host shows, and you might have the opportunity to volunteer at an event to learn the ins and outs of dog shows and meet mentors to steer you in the right direction.

THERAPY DOG

A therapy dog's primary work is comforting people. Therapy dogs provide comfort and affection to people in hospitals, retirement homes, and nursing homes, and with people who are in stressful situations, such as after a natural disaster. In schools, they work with people with learning disabilities. The therapeutic effects range from the feeling of well-being from canine companionship to relief from stress, lowering blood pressure, and raising spirits. Recently, there has been publicity about therapy dogs helping people with emotional and psychiatric disorders. Therapy dogs can help veterans returning from combat situations integrate back into civilian life.

Therapy dogs can be confused with service or assistant dogs, but there is a difference—service dogs are highly trained to directly assist disabled individuals and must meet rigorous requirements.

The main characteristic needed in a therapy dog is a people-loving personality. The ideal candidate is a dog who enjoys human contact and is content to be held in a lap and stroked. This dog must enjoy being fussed over and cooed to and...are you starting to get the picture? The typical Chihuahua is a good candidate!

There are some Chis who are one-person dogs and don't take to strangers, but with the right Chihuahua, therapy is a very rewarding activity. If your Chi is friendly, patient, and confident and has a relaxed, easygoing attitude in all situations, therapy may be for you. Your dog must be tolerant because many people will want to handle him in a therapy situation.

Service dogs are highly trained to directly assist disabled individuals and must meet rigorous requirements.

Make sure therapy is not only right for your dog, but right for you—if you don't enjoy people yourself, you aren't a good candidate. However, if you are outgoing and communicate well, then it can be highly rewarding.

Enrolling your Chihuahua in puppy and obedience classes is a good way to get started. You can't just arrive at a facility with your Chihuahua under your arm and expect to be welcomed in. Therapy dogs must meet certain standards. Your dog needs to be well-behaved and tested in a variety of awkward situations. Test requirements vary among organizations. Dogs who have the right attitude can be trained and tested through the AKC's CGC program. This program is often a prerequisite for many therapy organization programs. Good places to start your journey are the AKC's CGC page (www.akc.org/events/cgc) or Therapy Dogs International (www.tdi-dog.org).

TRAVELING WITH YOUR CHIHUAHUA

One of the biggest advantages of owning a Chihuahua is the fact that you can travel with him. Yes, they have many other charms, but what's not to like about taking your best friend with you everywhere? Traveling will expose your Chihuahua to many different experiences and is a wonderful fun way to socialize him.

CARRIER

Before you take your Chi anywhere, accustom him to the ubiquitous small-dog fashion accessory—the dog carrier. There are plenty of jokes about designer dog bags that are more expensive than the Chihuahua, but humor aside, the carrier is a necessary item for travel.

Feeding your Chi in the carrier is one way to accustom him to the bag. Teach him that his carrier is a comfy retreat, and he will come to look forward to travel.

TRAVELING BY CAR

Traveling in your automobile with your companion is safer with either a carrier, crate, or a seat belt attached to your Chi's harness. Specially made harnesses offer a safe way to travel, and many of them can be detached from the seat belt and used as a walking harness. Another option is a carrier that can be attached to the seat belt of the car. Whatever you choose, always secure your dog when he's in the car. That way, in case of an accident, he won't be flying through the air and injure himself or get loose and run off into dangerous traffic.

When traveling by car, have identification on your dog and the carrier. You should also carry a photo of your Chi with you in case of separation, so you have a way to identify him. Dogs may experience travel sickness when they travel by vehicle, which is usually a brief problem that with regular trips will subside.

TRAVELING BY AIR

Another advantage to traveling with a small dog is that he can fly with you in the cabin instead of in the cargo area. One stipulation is that your Chi must stay inside the carrier for the entire flight. Don't forget to check if the flight accepts dogs—sometimes an airline will have a limited number of allowed dogs on a flight and will have already reached the limit. You will pay for the dog to travel with you, and airlines differ on their rates and their regulations for allowing dogs onboard.

You must have the correct airline-approved carrier, and you need to accustom your dog to the carrier well before ever flying in one. You'll

A carrier is a necessary item for traveling with your Chi.

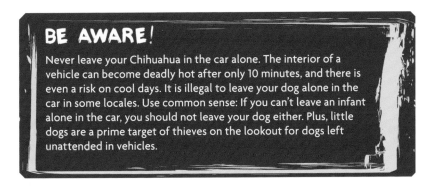

BE AWARE!

Never leave your Chihuahua in the car alone. The interior of a vehicle can become deadly hot after only 10 minutes, and there is even a risk on cool days. It is illegal to leave your dog alone in the car in some locales. Use common sense: If you can't leave an infant alone in the car, you should not leave your dog either. Plus, little dogs are a prime target of thieves on the lookout for dogs left unattended in vehicles.

need to get a health certificate from your veterinarian within 10 days of your journey. If you plan on an international flight, check if the country you are going to has quarantine regulations for animals arriving in their country.

PET-FRIENDLY LODGING

Finding a hotel/motel that will allow you bring your Chihuahua along can be challenging, although more lodgings are encouraging doggy visitors because of the popularity of vacationing with your pooch. Do an online search to find motel/hotels that accept dogs.

Do your part to keep the hotel/motels happy with canine visitors.

- Be courteous, so dogs will continue to be welcomed in the future. It is a privilege that some hotels allow dogs to stay with them, treat this privilege with respect.
- Always inquire ahead of time if well-behaved dogs are allowed.
- Pick up after your Chihuahua, and keep him confined in a crate if he can't hold his bladder.
- Make sure your Chi is accustomed to being alone in a crate and won't bark continuously and annoy other guests.
- Please don't sneak your doggy companion into the hotel.

RESOURCES

ASSOCIATIONS AND ORGANIZATIONS
BREED CLUBS
American Kennel Club (AKC)
5580 Centerview Drive
Raleigh, NC 27606
Telephone: (919) 233-9767
Fax: (919) 233-3627
E-Mail: info@akc.org
www.akc.org

Canadian Kennel Club (CKC)
89 Skyway Avenue, Suite 100
Etobicoke, Ontario M9W 6R4
Telephone: (416) 675-5511
Fax: (416) 675-6506
E-Mail: information@ckc.ca
www.ckc.ca

Federation Cynologique Internationale (FCI)
Secretariat General de la FCI
Place Albert 1er, 13
B – 6530 Thuin
Belqique
www.fci.be

The Kennel Club
1 Clarges Street
London
W1J 8AB
Telephone: 0870 606 6750
Fax: 0207 518 1058
www.the-kennel-club.org.uk

United Kennel Club (UKC)
100 E. Kilgore Road
Kalamazoo, MI 49002-5584
Telephone: (269) 343-9020
Fax: (269) 343-7037
E-Mail: pbickell@ukcdogs.com
www.ukcdogs.com

PET SITTERS
National Association of Professional Pet Sitters
15000 Commerce Parkway, Suite C
Mt. Laurel, New Jersey 08054
Telephone: (856) 439-0324
Fax: (856) 439-0525
E-Mail: napps@ahint.com
www.petsitters.org

Pet Sitters International
201 East King Street
King, NC 27021-9161
Telephone: (336) 983-9222
Fax: (336) 983-5266
E-Mail: info@petsit.com
www.petsit.com

RESCUE ORGANIZATIONS AND ANIMAL WELFARE GROUPS
American Humane Association (AHA)
63 Inverness Drive East
Englewood, CO 80112
Telephone: (303) 792-9900
Fax: 792-5333
www.americanhumane.org

American Society for the Prevention of Cruelty to Animals (ASPCA)
424 E. 92nd Street
New York, NY 10128-6804
Telephone: (212) 876-7700
www.aspca.org

The Humane Society of the United States (HSUS)
2100 L Street, NW
Washington DC 20037
Telephone: (202) 452-1100
www.hsus.org

Royal Society for the Prevention of Cruelty to Animals (RSPCA)
RSPCA Enquiries Service
Wilberforce Way, Southwater,
Horsham, West Sussex RH13 9RS
United Kingdom
Telephone: 0870 3335 999
Fax: 0870 7530 284
www.rspca.org.uk

SPORTS
International Agility Link (IAL)
Global Administrator: Steve
Drinkwater
E-Mail: yunde@powerup.au
www.agilityclick.com/~ial

The World Canine Freestyle Organization, Inc.
P.O. Box 350122
Brooklyn, NY 11235
Telephone: (718) 332-8336
Fax: (718) 646-2686
E-Mail: WCFODOGS@aol.com
www.worldcaninefreestyle.org

THERAPY
Delta Society
875 124th Ave, NE, Suite 101
Bellevue, WA 98005
Telephone: (425) 679-5500
Fax: (425) 679-5539
E-Mail: info@DeltaSociety.org
www.deltasociety.org

Therapy Dogs Inc.
P.O. Box 20227
Cheyenne WY 82003
Telephone: (877) 843-7364
Fax: (307) 638-2079
E-Mail: therapydogsinc@
qwestoffice.net
www.therapydogs.com

Therapy Dogs International (TDI)
88 Bartley Road
Flanders, NJ 07836
Telephone: (973) 252-9800
Fax: (973) 252-7171
E-Mail: tdi@gti.net
www.tdi-dog.org

TRAINING
Association of Pet Dog Trainers (APDT)
150 Executive Center Drive Box 35
Greenville, SC 29615
Telephone: (800) PET-DOGS
Fax: (864) 331-0767
E-Mail: information@apdt.com
www.apdt.com

International Association of Animal Behavior Consultants (IAABC)
565 Callery Road
Cranberry Township, PA 16066
E-Mail: info@iaabc.org
www.iaabc.org

National Association of Dog Obedience Instructors (NADOI)
PMB 369
729 Grapevine Hwy.
Hurst, TX 76054-2085
www.nadoi.org

VETERINARY AND HEALTH RESOURCES
Academy of Veterinary Homeopathy (AVH)
P.O. Box 9280
Wilmington, DE 19809
Telephone: (866) 652-1590
Fax: (866) 652-1590
www.theavh.org

American Academy of Veterinary Acupuncture (AAVA)
P.O. Box 1058
Glastonbury, CT 06033
Telephone: (860) 632-9911
Fax: (860) 659-8772
www.aava.org

American Animal Hospital Association (AAHA)
12575 W. Bayaud Ave.
Lakewood, CO 80228
Telephone: (303) 986-2800
Fax: (303) 986-1700
E-Mail: info@aahanet.org
www.aahanet.org/index.cfm

American College of Veterinary Internal Medicine (ACVIM)
1997 Wadsworth Blvd., Suite A
Lakewood, CO 80214-5293
Telephone: (800) 245-9081
Fax: (303) 231-0880
Email: ACVIM@ACVIM.org
www.acvim.org

American College of Veterinary Ophthalmologists (ACVO)
P.O. Box 1311
Meridian, ID 83860
Telephone: (208) 466-7624
Fax: (208) 466-7693
E-Mail: office09@acvo.com
www.acvo.com

American Holistic Veterinary Medical Association (AHVMA)
2218 Old Emmorton Road
Bel Air, MD 21015
Telephone: (410) 569-0795
Fax: (410) 569-2346
E-Mail: office@ahvma.org
www.ahvma.org

American Veterinary Medical Association (AVMA)
1931 North Meacham Road, Suite 100
Schaumburg, IL 60173-4360
Telephone: (847) 925-8070
Fax: (847) 925-1329
E-Mail: avmainfo@avma.org
www.avma.org

ASPCA Animal Poison Control Center
Telephone: (888) 426-4435
www.aspca.org

British Veterinary Association (BVA)
7 Mansfield Street
London
W1G 9NQ
Telephone: 0207 636 6541
Fax: 0207 908 6349
E-Mail: bvahq@bva.co.uk
www.bva.co.uk

Canine Eye Registration Foundation (CERF)
VMDB/CERF
1717 Philo Rd
P O Box 3007
Urbana, IL 61803-3007
Telephone: (217) 693-4800
Fax: (217) 693-4801
E-Mail: CERF@vmbd.org
www.vmdb.org

Orthopedic Foundation for Animals (OFA)
2300 NE Nifong Blvd
Columbus, Missouri 65201-3856
Telephone: (573) 442-0418
Fax: (573) 875-5073
Email: ofa@offa.org
www.offa.org

INDEX

Note: Boldfaced numbers indicate illustrations.

PHOTO CREDITS

ACKNOWLEDGMENTS

I want to thank Peggy Swager for her inspiration and her constant faith in me. The Olson/Swagers have become my second family.

I'd like to thank: Mom and Dad, Lonnie and Leslie Bollinger, Michele "Micki" Giroux, Linda Dillard, Cheryl Huffman, my Editors Stephanie Fornino and Heather Russell-Revesz.

ABOUT THE AUTHOR

Linda Bollinger has raised, trained, hunted with and shown dogs for over 25 years. She is the author of books and articles about purebred dogs, and was a canine newsletter editor for many years. Linda was a production artist for a publisher of canine books and magazines. She owns and operates a professional dog grooming shop. She lives in Palmer Lake, Colorado.

ABOUT ANIMAL PLANET™

Animal Planet™ is the only television network dedicated exclusively to the connection between humans and animals. The network brings people of all ages together by tapping into our fundamental fascination with animals through an array of fresh programming that includes humor, competition, drama, and spectacle from the animal kingdom.

ABOUT *DOGS 101*

The most comprehensive—and most endearing—dog encyclopedia on television, *DOGS 101* spotlights the adorable, the feisty and the unexpected. A wide-ranging rundown of everyone's favorite dog breeds—from the Dalmatian to Xoloitzcuintli—this series surveys a variety of breeds for their behavioral quirks, genetic history, most famous examples and wildest trivia. Learn which dogs are best for urban living and which would be the best fit for your family. Using a mix of animal experts, pop-culture footage and stylized dog photography, *DOGS 101* is an unprecedented look at man's best friend.